Celestial Transits

Or

Grah Gochar

Madhusudan Dusi

Preface

The Interpretation of a natal horoscope is an art that requires considerable skill. To interpret the horoscope, as it moves and unfolds through time, calls for even more skill. This is the reason, a good book that takes up the subject of astrological timing is valuable. The main objective of Astrology is to predict the future of the native with the help of his/her horoscope. For making accurate guidance it is necessary to make an analysis of certain factors.

The foremost and most important being the horoscope itself which should be analysed for various placements, aspects and conjunctions and certain Yogas or combinations. The second factor being the running Dasha system for the particular chart. The third factor is the Transit or the 'Gochar' of the current position planets with respect to the natal horoscope.

When a person comes with a query, first of all it should be analyzed that his/her query is related with which houses, signs and planets. The house and/or sign with, which the query is related is occupied by which planets and is receiving the aspects of which planets. The determination of the auspicious or inauspicious indications of that house shall be done by analysing the factors, such as house, house Lord and significators. Moon plays the most important and vital role in

Vedic Astrology and all the calculations start taking Moon and its Nakshatra as reference. The Dasha system starts with Star/Asterism occupied by the Moon. The Transit of the planets or the current position of planets with respect to the natal chart of the individual should also be taken in to account for a holistic approach and analysis. This book covers most of the factors dealing mainly with Transit or Gochar system. It is worth repeating that always a holistic approach is of paramount importance in analysing a horoscope, based on all the factors.

Contents

Chapter-1

Introduction

Every individual at some point of time is curious to know the forthcoming events of his/her life and its time of occurrence. Astrologer prepares an outline of the future of the individual by considering the 12 houses of the horoscope, combinations and strengths of planets etc. Then the astrologer tries to deduct the time when the indications could materialize. Giving occurrences of future events is a tedious task but timing of an event is more important.

Planets move on their path with their individual speeds around the Sun. In this way the planets complete their circumambulation around Sun by moving from one zodiac sign to other. When a person is born, the position of planets in various signs are indicated in the birth horoscope. After birth, the movement of planets in various signs indicates transit.

The natal horoscope indicates the permanent effects of planets on the life of individual but transit of planet signifies their influence at a particular time.

According to Vedic astrology, the fate of a person depends on the combined effect of natal horoscope, Dasha of planets and Transit.

Transits are the real-time physical astrological influences arising from the movement of planets, the connections made between the present placements by zodiacal sign and degree of the planets, luminaries and nodes at the time under consideration, and the placements of all the planets, luminaries, nodes, angles and houses in the birth chart(which indicate birth time positions) for the individual.

While a planet is aspecting, during its transit a celestial body in the horoscope, angle or node in the birth chart, the transit's effect could be experienced as the transiting body exerts a temporary influence, corresponding to its general nature and the type of aspect formed, upon the features of the personality, body and psychology governed by the aspected point in the birth chart.

In natal astrology quite large allowances are made for the effects of influence of the different types of aspects of planets, but their effects will be felt most strongly when they are exactly within just two degrees with respect to the natal position or directly aspecting the natal planets within two degrees, and the effect reduces considerably beyond two degrees. This applies right across the board for all the major aspects' types. It is perhaps advisable to allow three degrees for conjunctions and oppositions; two degrees for Kendra /Angles/Squares and Trikonas/Trines, and no more than one degree for sextiles and semi squares.

When transiting planets turn retrograde, they very commonly form in retrograde motion the same transiting aspect they would have made while in direct motion to a particular point in the birth chart. At this point, the same Issues highlighted in the life of the Individual affected during the first direct motion pass will be brought into focus again, but usually with a sense that there is more still to be done to resolve them. Then when the transiting planet involved turns direct once more and forms the same aspect in direct motion for a second and final time, the issues concerned would move in a direction towards indicating their final outcome as affected by the transit that has been ongoing.

Transits to the houses would exactly resemble natal chart placements of planets and luminaries in the houses. When a real-time planet or luminary occupies a zodiacal sign and degree placement that falls within the area of the zodiac spanned by a particular house in the birth chart, then the transit of that planet or luminary to that house is effective. Within three degrees of the cusp of the next house, the planet or luminary concerned will exhibit some influence in the next house.

While a celestial body or planet is transiting a particular house, the transit will be experienced as per the principles governed by the particular transiting body or planet exerting a temporary influence upon the area of life corresponding to the transited house. The nature of the influence would adjust the condition of the transited house in the birth chart while it lasts.

The transit system consists of appraising the positions of the nine planets at a particular time for which the good or bad effects are to be ascertained together with the planetary position and the rising sign in the birth chart.

While analysing the results of transit, it should be ascertained whether a particular planet is favourable or adverse in the horoscope. As per experience it is known that a planet that appears benefic in the horoscope initially need not indicate favourable results because in reality may not be benefic because of either its functional position or ownership in the chart or malefic aspects. For example if a person has Vrishabha Lagna or Taurus ascendant and Jupiter is posited in 10th house of the horoscope, in which case it is known that

Jupiter in 10th house of natural zodiac indicates good results but experience does not corroborate it. Because for Taurus ascendant, Jupiter is 8th and 11th lord of the chart, therefore it indicates adverse results. Similarly, planets have to be evaluated for other ascendants as well.

Functional status of planets for all 12 Lagnas or ascendants.

1. Mesha or Aries: Sun, Mars and Jupiter are benefic and Moon, Mercury, Venus and Saturn are malefic.
2. Vrishabha or Taurus: Sun, Mars, Mercury and Saturn are benefic, Venus is neutral, Moon and Jupiter are malefic.
3. Mithuna or Gemini: Venus is benefic, Mercury and Moon are neutral, Sun, Mars, Jupiter and Saturn are malefic.
4. Karka or Cancer: Moon, Mars and Jupiter are benefic, Sun and Saturn are neutral, Mercury and Venus are malefic.
5. Simha or Leo: Sun and Mars are benefic, Moon, Jupiter and Saturn are neutral, Venus and Mercury are malefic.
6. Kanya or Virgo: Venus is benefic, Sun, Mercury and Saturn are neutral, Jupiter, Mars and Moon are malefic.
7. Tula or Libra: Mars, Mercury, Venus and Saturn are benefic, Sun, Moon and Jupiter are malefic.
8. Vrischika or Scorpio: Sun, Moon and Jupiter are benefic, Mars and Saturn are neutral, Venus and Mercury are malefic.

9. Dhanu or Sagittarius: Sun and Mars are benefic, Moon and Jupiter are neutral, Mercury, Venus and Saturn are malefic.

10. Makara or Capricorn: Mercury, Venus and Saturn are benefic, Sun is neutral, Moon, Mars and Jupiter are malefic.

11. Kumbha or Aquarius: Sun, Mars, Venus and Saturn are benefic, Mercury is neutral, Moon and Jupiter are malefic

12. Meena or Pisces: Mars and Moon are benefic, Jupiter is neutral, Saturn, Venus, Mercury and Sun are malefic.

It should be noted that planets which are designated as benefic, neutral or malefic would tend to be so but only to a certain extent and they would also indicate quite opposing effect which would depend on multiple factors, such as owning of the second house/sign which could be positive or negative. The planets which have two signs would have a tendency to indicate those results which are indicated more by their ownership with the Moolatrikona Sign and to a lesser extent by the other sign. Thus for every position there would be both positive as well as negative indications, the extent of which should be carefully judged.

Chapter 2

Transit Principles

Vedic astrology presents innumerable methods of interpreting results of transits which have been enumerated by classical texts. Generally speaking, when transiting planets come into Conjunction, Opposition, 6th / 8th position (Shasta-Ashtaka), or Trine position with any natal planetary placements, the transiting planets create an energy which indicates some positive effects and some negative indications. There are, however, some basic guidelines to remember when arriving at transit results.

1. Transiting planets, which may be favourable according to general rules, may not indicate favourable results. This could be due to unfavourable placements in relationship to the birth planets regardless of favourable transit position from the birth moon.

2. When Jupiter transits through the exact degrees of a natal planet, it enhances matters in the house owned by that planet. For example, Jupiter, when it passes over the planetary lord of the 5th house, promotes children and all aspects related to children.

3. Depending on the nature of the planets involved, strong or weak, positive or negative indications can be found and expected when a transiting planet enters into opposition with a natal planet.

4. Positive aspect between the natal and transiting Jupiter indicates positive results.

5. When a transiting planet exerts its influences on a particular sign, the owner of that house also receives the influence of the transiting planet.

6. Whenever adverse results are indicated, Mars will be transiting the Lagna, the Moon, the Sun, or the houses related to the areas of affliction or it will be in opposition to these houses.

7. When Saturn conjoins or is in opposition to the Sun or the Moon it indicates adverse effects. Generally, the Moon indicates emotional issues and the Sun indicates government related or official matters.

8. When Rahu & Ketu pass over Saturn, sudden and unexpected developments could take place.

9. The Sun's transit of the Sun sign or opposition to it could indicate difficulties and troubles.

10. If the Moon transits in favourable aspects to benevolent planets, indications would be good.

11. When Dasha/Antardasha/Bhukti are operating, if such planets in transit are in exaltation, own house, etc., it indicates good results, and negative results when such planets go to debilitated signs.

12. A benefic planet becomes more beneficial when it retrogrades. Whereas a malefic planet becomes more malefic when it retrogrades.

13. A benefic planet transiting a benefic house will not indicate good results if conjunct or powerfully aspected by negative planets. Similarly, negative planets will not be as negative when conjunct or aspected by a benevolent planet.

14. All planets become capable of giving positive indications when they transit the 11th house provided they are not afflicted by malefic association, combustion, or opposition, etc.

Timing through Planets' Nakshatra 'Pada or Charan' Transits

The Nakshatra Padas are very important concept in Vedic astrology, because they are mapped to the Navamsas. The Navamsa division is vital as it indicates the sum total of previous Janma Karma and how it could affect the good and bad events in this life. So in a way, our freedom of actions and manifestation of results are bounded by the past life Karmas. For instance, if an individual changes his/her job, what they did in their previous workplaces will always follow them like a shadow, if one did a good job, people will have good impression about them, else, one can be in troubles often. Similarly Navamsa is a very important division in Vedic astrology.

The Rashi placement of Planets in Navamsas indicate the subtle energies the Planets are imbibed with. When a Planet is placed in Mesha Rashi in natal chart, the Planet is influenced by the effects of Mesha Rashi, however, the effects are broad and are a combination of many subtle indications. However, when the Planet occupies Mesha Navamsa, the effect of Mesha on the Planet is very clear and focused. This principle is similar to the concept of Day and Hora. For instance, when a work needs to be performed on a Sunday, if it can't be done, Narada Purana suggests that the same work can be performed in Sun's hora on any day, this implies that, on any day, the effects of Sun is very strong in its Hora, of course, there will be some difference in strength depending on the Day on which the Hora occurs.

Analysing Planets' movement through Rashis or Signs is important but it should be noted that these transits are required to be minutely looked at and analysed based on their movement through various Nakshatra Padas or Navamsas.

When Jupiter transits the natal 9th lord, it can indicate rise in fortune, good luck and success in some important endeavour, this can be further strengthened by observing and noting that when Jupiter is transiting close to the natal longitude of the 9th lord. If the Nakshatra Pada of the 9th lord is known, by observing the movement of Jupiter in that Nakshatra Pada, it is possible to arrive at a more precise timing of the event.

The Trines of the transiting Planets can also be looked at as those points are also closely connected to the transiting planet, because the Trinal Nakshatras always have the same Nakshatra Lord. For instance, say, that the 9th lord occupies Krittika Nakshatra, which is Sun's Nakshatra, 3rd Pada. When Jupiter transits Krittika Nakshatra 3rd Pada, it will get connected with the Planet occupying the 3rd Pada of other Sun's Nakshatras i.e., Uttara-Phalguni and Uttarashada.

Find the Planet owning the Nakshatra being transited. There will invariably be some positive or negative indication pertaining to this Nakshatra Lord, depending on the transiting

Planet. For instance, when Jupiter is transits Mars' Nakshatra, it can indicate positive results pertaining to the ownership, placement and yogas of Mars in the Natal Chart.

The Navatara Chakra should be cast from Moon's natal position. When Jupiter, Venus or any functionally benefic planet transits through the good Tara (Nakshatra) i.e., 2nd Nakshatra-Sampat, 4th Nakshatra-Kshema, 6th Nakshatra-Sadhaka, 8th Nakshatra-Mitra, 9th Nakshatra-Atimitra, positive events can be indicated, actually the 9th Nakshatra or Tara is neutral, similarly when malefic planets transit through an inauspicious star i.e., 1st Nakshatra-Janma, 3rd Nakshatra-Vipat, 5th Nakshatra-Pratyak, 7th Nakshatra-Vadha, inauspicious events can be indicated, here again the Janma Nakshatra is neutral.

Observe the Navamsa in which the Planet is transiting, it has the ability to indicate the results pertaining to the house coinciding with the Navamsa sign in the Rashi chart. For instance, when Jupiter transits through Dhanu Rasi and Mesha Navamsa for a Dhanu Lagna native, it has the ability to indicate 5th house related events as Mesha is identical with the 5th house in the Rashi chart of an individual with Dhanu Lagna.

When the transiting Planet conjoins with a natal Planet in the Navamsa, then it has the ability to indicate effects pertaining to its ownership, placement and Yog. For instance, when Jupiter transits through Dhanu Rashi, Simha Navamsa for a Dhanu Lagna individual, with Simha Navamsa containing Mercury, the effects and indications of Mercury i.e., 7th house, 10th house ownership and 9th house placement could get indicated, as Mercury owns the 7th and 10th houses for a Dhanu lagna and ninth house takes the Simha Rashi. This can indicate rise in fortune, promotions, betterment in relationships, business etc. The indications would be even stronger, when Jupiter transits over or aspect the Planet in the Natal Chart. For instance, if Jupiter aspects Mercury occupying Simha Rasi from Dhanu, indicating the likelihood of the events to be even higher.

Although the birth Moon sign, also known as Moon lagna, is of prime importance for determining the effect of transit, the transits can also be analysed from the Lagna.

Chapter 3

Judging a Transit

The ancient scripts have recommended for the use of sign where Moon is situated in the natal Horoscope to start or initiate transit combinations. The situation of a transiting planet at a particular time from Moon sign indicates the result of transit for that time.

The three types of Lagnas or ascendants, are popular in astrology. Lagna or ascendant, Moon ascendant and Sun ascendant are also considered for various studies. It is critical to find which ascendant, the Lagna or ascendant, Moon or Sun should be seen for results and indications of transit. All ascendants signify different matters. Lagna ascendant signifies personality, Moon indicates mind and Sun represents the soul. The individual is made by the combination of all three. The soul cannot assert itself without body. Body is controlled by mind and mind controls all senses and organs of body. Therefore importance of Moon ascendant is uppermost in judging and analysing transits and dasha systems. Transit analysis should be taken up with both the Lagna or birth ascendant and the Moon ascendant.

The reference for the Dasha system is also Moon, where the Nakshatra under which Moon is posited is taken as the starting reference for calculations of Dashas. The importance of a Tithi is also due to Moon. The constellation of a day is also seen from Moon. The constellation where Moon is posited on a day is regarded as constellation for that day.

Ashtakavarga system also deals with transits. The Ashtakavarga is formed by combination of ascendant and 7 planets, where Rahu and Ketu (North Node and South Node) are not considered. Ashtakavarga gives indications about the good-bad situations of planets.

Transit works under Mahadasha (Major Period) and Antardasha (Sub Period). If the operating Dasha- Antardasha are of adverse planets but transit is favourable the individual will not have good results. Transit indicates about the present situation of planets with respect to the position of planets in natal horoscope. A planet which is well placed in birth horoscope will indicate good results as soon as it comes in favourable situation in transit, but the planet which is adverse in birth horoscope will not indicate good results when it comes in favourable position in transit. When the transiting planets come in the same sign and degrees of its position in birth horoscope, their results are clearly visible.

Suppose Mercury is posited in Virgo at 10° in natal horoscope in exaltation, when Mercury comes next in transit in Virgo at 10°, its good or bad results could be seen. In this way transiting planets remain under the influence of natal planets and their position.

If a planet is exalted or in own sign in birth horoscope, it will not indicate bad results when it comes in an adverse position in transit. The results of transit are based on position of planets in birth horoscope.

Transit is also dependent on the Janma Tara and there on, i.e. the Star in which the Moon was posited at the time of birth. The 2nd, 4th, 6th, 8th Stars or Taras from the Janma Tara are beneficial, thus planets transiting these Stars tend to indicate positive attributes during their transit with respect to the attributes of the corresponding house. Similarly, the 3rd, 5th, 7th Stars or Taras from the Janma Tara are malefic, thus planets transiting these Stars tend to indicate malefic attributes with respect to the attributes of the corresponding house. The first Star or Tara and the 9th Star or Tara are neutral in nature and hence their transit effects and indications are also neutral for all transiting planets.

The result of transit is arrived at by combining the results of all transiting planets. The result of a single planet is not important.

In the study of transit, all combinations of natal and transitory planets are not important but conjunctions and oppositions are significant and relatively conjunction is more important. Certain houses of the horoscope are important. The transit of Sun, Saturn, Jupiter and Mars over these places gives visible results. The cusp of birth ascendant, middle position of 10th house, natal Sun, Jupiter and Moon are important. Transit over these locations gives significant results.

The transits that have the most dramatic and marked influences are those which reinforce natal aspects and involve the same planets. For example, a natal square between Mars and Mercury indicates a tendency towards irritability and mental vehemence. Thus, whenever transiting Mars or Mercury makes a square, conjunction, or opposition to natal Mars or Mercury, the individual could experience unusual irritation and mental annoyance. This is because transiting Mercury or Mars is reinforcing natal stress aspect involving these two planets. When a planet nears the final degree of a house cusp, it often gives powerful results relating to the fundamental nature of the transit.

The meaning of a transit depends upon the position of the transiting planet in relation to the natal horoscope, the aspects it makes to the natal planets, and its position in the natal houses.

To interpret a transit, first look to the sign and house position the planet is transiting. These indicate the practical affairs of life to be directly activated by the transiting planet. The natal houses ruled by the transiting planet should also be considered, as well as the house or houses of which the planet is the exalted ruler.

Next, consider the aspects made by the transiting planet to any natal planet during its transit through a house. The affairs ruled by the natal planet receiving the transit will influence the affairs of that house.

The type of aspect being made, the sign and houses ruled by the transiting planet, and the natal planet that is being aspected, along with the signs and houses the natal planet rules, must be considered in determining the effects of a transit.

The exalted ownerships of the transiting and natal planets and the houses holding the signs of these exalted ownerships must also be considered. Exalted ownerships indicate where the power behind an event or action signified by the transit originates or is generated. For example, if Venus is transiting the natal fifth house, the individual could experience pleasurable social, romantic, and aesthetic activities. To determine the source of these romantic or social stimulations, look to the houses where Vrishabha/Taurus, Tula/Libra and Meena/Pisces are found in the natal horoscope. (Venus rules Vrishabha/Taurus and Tula/Libra and is exalted in Meena/Pisces).

Also, if Venus is making a trine aspect to natal Mars while transiting the natal fifth house, consider the sign and house position of natal Mars and the houses where Mesha/Aries, Vrischika/Scorpio, and Makara/Capricorn are placed, for Mars rules Mesha/Aries and Vrischika/Scorpio and is exalted in Makara/Capricorn.

These and such factors could be overwhelmingly confusing unless their relative importance is considered. Transits to the birth chart of individual will often alter this individual's perceptions and outward projections. The transiting planets linking in to his or her birth chart, alters both how he or she comes across to other people and how he or she perceives any emotional situation and life in general.

Another factor is, exaltation or debilitation does not always indicate positive or negative attributes respectively. Exaltation and/or debilitation merely indicates the powerful or powerless state of the planet. If a planet is functionally malefic and debilitated also, it does not become more malefic, instead it is in a powerless state to indicate much maleficence. Similarly, if a planet is functionally benefic and debilitated, it indicates a state of being in less powerful position to indicate much beneficence.

Planets give positive indications when they transit through the following houses of the natal chart, with respect to the Moon Sign of the natal chart.

Planet	Good Houses
Sun	3, 6, 10, 11
Moon	1, 3, 6, 7, 10, 11
Mars	3, 6, 11
Mer	2, 4, 6, 7, 8, 10, 11
Jup	2, 5, 7, 9, 11
Ven	1, 2, 3, 4, 5, 8, 9, 10, 12
Sat	3, 6, 11
Rahu/Ketu	3, 6, 10, 11

Planets give negative indications when they transit through the following houses of the natal chart, with respect to the Moon Sign of the natal chart.

Planet	Good Houses
Sun	1, 2, 4, 5, 7, 8, 9, 12
Moon	2, 4, 5, 8, 9, 12
Mars	1, 2, 4, 5, 7, 8, 9, 10, 12
Mer	1, 3, 5, 9, 12
Jup	1, 3, 4, 6, 8, 10, 12
Ven	6, 7, 11
Sat	1, 2, 4, 5, 7, 8, 9, 10, 12
Rahu/Ketu	1, 2, 4, 5, 7, 8, 9, 12

Transit of Sun on 10th house of natal horoscope is important. Transit of Sun gives the indications of house of its transit. When Sun moves over natal Saturn, exactly around 2 to 4 days either side of natal Saturn's position, it indicates problems and failure. Every year these days are fixed, therefore it is advantageous to remember it.

Transit of Venus in 1, 2, 5, 7, 9 houses from Lagna or Ascendant is benefic. At other places it is not important with respect to Lagna. Transiting Venus on Lagna gives peace of mind, health would be generally good, days would be joyous and full of entertainment. Venus in 2nd house gives nearness to family members, money transactions could be favourable, would have a pleasant mood, of course for all these positive indications natal Venus position should be benefic. Venus in 5th house indicates luxuries. Transit of Venus on 7th house indicates marital bliss. Venus on 9th house confers success in job or business. Transit of all planets can be judged with respect to both the Lagna of the natal chart or the Moon sign of the natal chart, where the importance of the later is higher.

Chapter 4

Vedha or Obstructions to Transits

When a planet transits through a benefic house of the natal chart and at the same time another planet is transiting on an obstructing or badhaka house the benefic results of the transit are converted into malefic ones to some extent and the extent would depend on the exactness of the obstruction and aspect, and on those particular days when the transiting obstruction takes place and not always. This behaviour of planets is called Vedha. The Vedha houses are taken with respect to the natal Moon Sign, same as transit of the planets.

Vedha stands for obstruction. In order that an obstruction is not caused to the conveying of the benefic result, this specified Vedha house must be free from occupation by another transiting planet. Vedhas should be carefully analysed along with transit effects to get a holistic view of the chart, which of course comes in importance only next to the Dasha system.

The transits and the corresponding Vedhas for all the seven planets, excluding Rahu and Ketu are mentioned here. The transits and Vedhas of Rahu and Ketu follow the same pattern as that of Sun.

Vedha houses of planets:-

Sun

House	1	2	3	4	5	6
Transit	Neg	Neg	Pos	Neg	Neg	Pos
Vedha	--	--	9th	--	--	12th

House	7	8	9	10	11	12
Transit	Neg	Neg	Neg	Pos	Pos	Neg
Vedha	--	--	--	4th	5th	--

Neg – Negative effect; Pos -- Positive effect
-- indicates no Vedha
Benefic houses or houses with Positive indications for Sun's transit are 3rd, 6th, 10th and 11th houses.

The Vedha houses for Sun's transit are 4th, 5th, 9th, and 12th. Thus there are no Vedha for Sun's transit in 1st, 2nd, 4th, 5th, 7th, 8th, 9th and 12th houses, that is to say any planets transit-presence in these houses would not cause Vedha to the Sun's transit, but it is pertinent to note that, Sun's transit in 1st, 2nd, 4th, 5th, 7th, 8th, 9th and 12th houses is negative and if there could be a Vedha to these houses, then the negative effect of Sun's transit to these houses could get lesser. Thus Vedhas cause reduction of both Positive and Negative effects

Also, if the Sun is transiting in the 3rd house from natal Moon, it has a positive effect, but we can see from the table that 3rd house has a Vedha from 9th house, which means, if there is a transiting planet in the 9th house from natal Moon while the Sun is transiting the 3rd house, there will be Vedha from the planet in the 9th house and due to this, the positive effect of Sun's transit in the 3rd house would be lesser.

Similarly Sun is auspicious on 6th house but it will lose its beneficence if a planet is present in 12th house, which would cause Vedha, and If Sun is in transiting in 10th house, a planet's presence in 4th house would create a Vedha and if Sun is on 11th house, a planet in 5th house will cause Vedha or obstruction and weaken the positive effect of Sun. An exception to Sun's transit effects, is it does not have Vedha from Saturn. Similarly the transits and their corresponding Vedhas should be ascertained and analysed.

Moon

House	1	2	3	4	5	6
Transit	Pos	Neg	Pos	Neg	Neg	Pos
Vedha	--	8th	9th	--	--	12th

House	7	8	9	10	11	12
Transit	Pos	Neg	Neg	Pos	Pos	Neg
Vedha	--	2nd	--	4th	5th	--

Moon has positive transit effect when it transits the 1st, 3rd, 6th, 7th, 10th and 11th houses from its own natal position. Also, Moon has Vedha from all twelve houses that is, any planet present in any of the twelve houses would cause Vedha to Moon's transiting house. Here again, a Vedha to a Negative effect house would reduce the negativity and similarly the positivity of a positive Moon's transit also would reduce by a Vedha if any planet is present in the Vedha causing house, at the same time there would be no Vedha if no planet is present in the Vedha causing house.

The only exception to Moon's transit is Mercury's presence in any of the Vedha causing houses does not give a Vedha to the Moon's transiting house.

Mars

House	1	2	3	4	5	6
Transit	Neg	Neg	Pos	Neg	Neg	Pos
Vedha	7th	8th	9th	10th	--	12th

House	7	8	9	10	11	12
Transit	Neg	Neg	Neg	Neg	Pos	Neg
Vedha	1st	2nd	--	4th	5th	--

Mars' transit in 3rd, 6th and 11th houses from natal Moon position indicates positive effects and any other planet's transit in 1st, 2nd, 4th, 5th, 7th, 8th,

9th, 10th, 12th houses creates Vedha thus reducing both the positive or negative effect depending on the Vedha house.

Mercury

House	1	2	3	4	5	6
Transit	Neg	Pos	Neg	Pos	Neg	Pos
Vedha	--	--	9th	--	--	12th

House	7	8	9	10	11	12
Transit	Pos	Pos	Neg	Pos	Pos	Neg
Vedha	1st	--	3rd	--	5th	--

Mercury's transit in 2nd, 4th, 6th, 7th, 8th, 10th, 11th houses from natal Moon indicates positive effects but if another planet is transiting in 1st, 3rd, 5th, 9th and 12th houses, the positive effect gets reduced due to Vedha. The exception to Mercury's transit is Moon's transit in Vedha houses does not create a Vedha.

Jupiter

House	1	2	3	4	5	6
Transit	Neg	Pos	Neg	Neg	Pos	Neg
Vedha	--	8th	--	10th	--	12th

House	7	8	9	10	11	12
Transit	Pos	Neg	Pos	Neg	Pos	Neg
Vedha	1st	--	3rd	4th	--	6th

Jupiter indicates positive effects while transiting in 2nd, 5th, 7th, 9th and 11th houses from natal Moon position. Jupiter gets Vedha from any planet's transit in all houses except 1st house and 6th house. Also, either the positivity or the negativity of the Jupiter's transit does not reduce much due to Vedhas. Jupiter is considered the most beneficial planet in most of the combinations except a few, that is the reason the Vedhas to Jupiter's transit does not cause much negative effect to the positive transits as well as the negative transits.

Venus

House	1	2	3	4	5	6
Transit	Pos	Pos	Pos	Pos	Pos	Neg
Vedha	7th	--	--	--	11th	--

House	7	8	9	10	11	12
Transit	Neg	Pos	Pos	Neg	Pos	Pos
Vedha	--	--	--	--	--	6th

The transit of Venus gives positive effects while transiting in 1st, 2nd, 3rd, 4th, 5th, 8th, 9th, 11th, 12th houses from the natal Moon position. Planets transiting in all the houses cause Vedha to the transiting Venus. Venus generally indicates all positive things in life and negative effects in some cases. Here the positivity or the negativity gets affected by the corresponding planet's transit in the Vedha causing house.

Saturn

House	1	2	3	4	5	6
Transit	Neg	Neg	Pos	Neg	Neg	Pos
Vedha	7th	8th	9th	--	--	12th

House	7	8	9	10	11	12
Transit	Neg	Neg	Neg	Neg	Pos	Neg
Vedha	1st	2nd	--	4th	5th	--

Saturn's transit in 3rd, 6th and 11th houses from natal Moon position indicates positive effects and any other planet's transit in 1st, 2nd, 4th, 5th, 7th, 8th, 9th, and 12th houses creates Vedha thus reducing both the positive or negative effect depending on the Vedha house. The transit behaviour and effects of Mars and Saturn are similar.

Chapter 5

Transits Relative to Lagna/Ascendant

The basic foundation of a horoscope is the Lagna or the Ascendant, which signifies almost all aspects of life such as personality, direction of thoughts, general well-being, prosperity etc. Transits are analysed with respect to natal Moon Sign/Rashi generally, but the transit of planets through the Lagna or Ascendant and also through various points are also to be analysed in a horoscope with respect to lagna or Ascendant is covered which can always be expanded further with more details in depth.

Transit of Sun

When Sun transits **through the Lagna**, the individual would feel and get sudden burst of energy and enthusiasm, renewing his/her confidence to face the world to impress everyone around. They will have a favourable time to take control for gain, deal with their opponents in a diplomatic way to win them over. The transit represents new beginnings in many ways for the individual, where he/she can restart things which they attempted earlier and could not achieve their objectives or finish what they started. Also this period may not be much suitable or not a good time to resolve martial conflicts. One must attend to their health issues and personality matters.

Sextile to a House: When Sun transits sextile to a house, that is when it is 60° away from a house, it has sextile aspect on the house. During this transit, the individual may have to take the role of being a leader or an authority and undertake important assignments which could have impact on everyone around. When the person has to work along with others during this period that could benefit him/her. There could be social, enjoyment with one's colleagues and friends and there could be well deserved respect and recognition.

Square to a House: When Sun transits Square or Kendra to a house that is at 90° to a house under consideration, the individual should take care of health, avoid conflict with others as there could be a high likelihood of a problem, clash, etc. thus it is best to avoid it. Relationships with superiors and persons with authority in job or business may become strained resulting in disturbance, anxiety and worries.

Trine to a House: When Sun transits Trine or Kona to a house that is at 120° to a house under consideration, this period is a good time to get cooperation from others, to feel energetic and to enjoy. Hard-work will be rewarding during this period. Good scope for expansion in one's profession or business. There could be journeys to relax and vigour will be favourable. Opponents would not able to win over the individual during this transit. Relations with superiors will be cordial and the individual will be rewarded and helped by them for work and attitude.

Opposite to a House: When Sun transits a house opposite to the one under consideration that is the seventh house from a house under consideration, the negative attributes of the house become more dominant and this period indicates a volatile and dynamic period one could go through. During this period there could be some unexpected and sudden negative circumstances which could come to the fore and with relatively lesser possibility of some positive happenings. One should be cautious about dealings with others. Group working and partnerships would fetch good results and will pay up. Partnership will be beneficial and a success and can expect some gains in consultation with others.

Transit of Moon

When Moon transits **through the Lagna**, emotions and sentiments would be driven on top of everything an individual does or thinks, which calls for extreme cautiousness in dealing with everything, every situation and every person.

Depending on the benefic or malefic aspects on the transit Moon situations can either be positive or negative, which would depend on the strength of Moon. Cordial relations with opposite sex forming relations of love and friendship are possible and this would also be a good time to propose love to one's sexual partner. However, control of emotions even in the matters of love is recommended during this transit.

Sextile to a House: When Moon transits sextile to a house, that is when it is 60° away from a house, it has sextile aspect on the house. During this period close associations with loved ones who may be friends, relations and opposite sex, and others will respond positively. The relations can be strengthened. Sweet speech could remove the differences with people having strained relations. This would be a good time for achieving and completing group tasks, public appearance and dealings and to get cooperation from others. Relations with others would be cordial.

Square to a House: When Moon transits a Square or Kendra to a house that is at 90° to a house under consideration, this period may not be a happy period for dealing with others, can create conflict causing depression and loss. The individual should not get emotional during this transit to avoid differences with his/her loved ones, friends and relations. Taking any decision emotionally at this time may be counter-productive.

Trine to a House: When Moon transits Trine or Kona to a house that is at 120° to a house under consideration, during this period contacts with others will be warm and emotional which could be quite lasting. The individual would be helpful to others with good level of understanding nature. He/she would have cordial and helpful and enjoyable relations with everyone in general and particularly with the opposite sex who could respond in a similar manner. There would be chance of gain through friends and opposite sex. Public work and strangers also could be of help during this time.

Opposite to a House: When Moon transits a house opposite to the one under consideration that is the seventh house from a house under consideration, this time indicates that this would be a good emotional time, when one will be closely involved with someone in a opposite sex. It is better to hear and adopt some positive opinions and narratives of others. Any deals, negotiations and contracts if possible should be avoided from being finalised during this time.

Transit of Mercury

When Mercury transits **through the Lagna**, this would be a favourable time for negotiations, contracts and business dealings. There would gains through correspondence, being receptive to others and the individual will generally have a sharp and clear mind during this time. This would be a time to work and should avoid relaxing too much. Travelling will be more than usual but could be gainful. This time things and situations be more or less smoother. Mental pursuits will be favourable.

Sextile to a House: When Mercury transits sextile to a house, that is when it is 60° away from a house, it has sextile aspect on the house. This is a good period for travelling, mental work, making or initiating important communication and expressing, for business and negotiations etc. Gains can be expected during this time through some vital communications. Relatives, friends and acquaintances would be congenial. This is a positive time for settling down disputes if any, and to reach an agreement. Contacts with people would be meaningful. Trading, selling and buying for personal reasons would be profitable, also profitable for the purpose of commercial or business intentions.

Square to a House: When Mercury transits a Square or Kendra to a house that is at 90° to a house under consideration, during this time one should not expect everyone to agree with them as there could always be some difference of opinion, thus it is advisable to be slow in expressing oneself and with a calm approach and should listen to others. Generally there would be gain from communication with this approach. Make plans for doing work, do not enter into excessive correspondence and exchange of views.

Trine to a House: When Mercury transits Trine or Kona to a house that is at 120° to a house under consideration, this period would be good for intellectual discussions and communications, short business travels would be gainful. Overall this is a good period to attend conferences, negotiations, to reach an agreement and well thought out compromises. People will listen to one's viewpoints with intent.

Opposite to a House: When Mercury transits a house opposite to the one under consideration that is the seventh house from a house under consideration, this could be a period of meetings, conversation which could be useful if one does not get too angry and vociferous. This time would be favourable period for consulting lawyers, doctor or business specialist etc. Communications will be favourable. The individual may face some legal contest or negotiations.

Transit of Venus

When Venus transits **through the Lagna**, this a generally positive time. A most favourable time for personal relations. One can express their love and would receive affection in return, for the settlement of disputes and differences of opinions with people and loved ones. A contact with new person, beloved or friend. Get-togethers, entertainments will be source of joy and gain. A good period for financial gain.

Sextile to a House: When Venus transits sextile to a house, that is when it is 60° away from a house, it has sextile aspect on the house. This period one would relax and enjoy with their loved ones and friends. Opponents will become congenial to you, disputes can be settled.
Your relations with all and people around you will be congenial. A love relation if started during this period would go a long way happily. Meeting with people will be beneficial. Get-togethers, parties, entertainments will open new environments to the individual's advantage, as they would make favourable impression upon others.

Square to a House: When Venus transits a Square or Kendra to a house that is at 90° to a house under consideration, this would be an excellent trine for entertainments, love, pleasure and joy. The individual would be generous, more affectionate and people around him/her will like them. Social gatherings will be favourable, happy relations with lovers, beloved people, relations, friends, and especially with children, A good financial period. Changes for good at home and surroundings are indicated.

Trine to a House: When Venus transits Trine or Kona to a house that is at 120° to a house under consideration, this is an excellent trine for entertainments, love, pleasure and joy. The person will be generous, more affectionate and people around him/her would be affectionate. Social gatherings would be favourable, happy relations with loved ones and with the opposite sex, friends and especially with children. This time would be a good financial period. Changes for good at home and surroundings would be indicated.

Opposite to a House: When Venus transits a house opposite to the one under consideration that is the seventh house from a house under consideration, this would be a good period for smooth relations, a marriage or love relation would be smooth. Arguments are best avoided during this period. Those persons who are difficult to be handled would be easier to handle during this time. The individual would enjoy the company of the opposite sex.

Transit of Mars

When Mars transits **through the Lagna**, one should careful in most of the things they do, in their daily lives. The individual would be relatively more comfortable during this period if he/she is cooperative with and accommodative to others else there could be mental disturbances. All conflicts are best to be handled diplomatically during this time as little things could go out of control easily. The person would be energetic and dashing during this transit. Joint work in any direction will pay nicely. Team work is advised with cooperation else there could be anger and disputes. Revengeful actions should be avoided during this time. Control over senses and staying within disciplined parameters should be adhered to while travelling especially of driving. Taking care of one's health is a must by regulating one's diet. Over work and straining should be avoided. Avoid use of sharp instruments and fire arms, even though one could be bold. Rash temperament, obstinacy, bossing over others are best avoided during this time.

Sextile to a House: When Mars transits sextile to a house, that is when it is 60° away from a house, it has sextile aspect on the house. This is a good and favourable period for group working

Leading teams in to action. The individual would have high levels of energy during this transit which should be put to constructive use. Colleagues and friends would listen to the person and will be cooperative. The individual would be impulsive, which should be controlled and physically strong and will attract others. Fruitful actions would bear good results. A good period for the kind of work which involves high levels of energy and stamina.

Square to a House: When Mars transits a Square or Kendra to a house that is at 90° to a house under consideration, during this transit there could be differences with wife, friends, relations and opposite sex, but with calmness and self, assertive attitude, can solve them, avoid those issues. Team work may not be much favourable hence care should be taken. It is not advisable to enter in to any type of agreements during this transit time. This would not be the time to get involved in any dangerous works involving any risks. This transit may indicate some injuries and accident, care of health against blood pressure, illness and minor infections and irritation be taken.

Trine to a House: When Mars transits Trine or Kona to a house that is at 120° to a house under consideration, this transit time would be a good period for sports and games players. The individual would be vigorous in health and thus they can deal with others with self-assurance and without aggressive action. They would be capable to take definite decisions to expand their activities. Any dogmatic views and working during this transit could prove counter-productive and may not be favourable, rather one should associate with others to share the views. In case Mars is afflicted in natal chart and also during this transit one's health and relations can be ill affected.

Opposite to a House: When Mars transits a house opposite to the one under consideration that is the seventh house from a house under consideration, open enemies and conflicts are indicated during this transit and direct confrontation with one's life partners and loved ones can take place. The business in partnership can be a problem and there could be some differences and issues to deal with during this time. One may have to bear the dominance of others to avoid any struggle and attempts should be made with calm mind and try and reconcile such situations to avoid separation, divorce etc. Team work would be generally favourable. Care should be taken against falls, injuries and accidents. Steps such as avoiding sports which could cause injuries, use of sharp instruments and firearms can be avoided during this time.
Transit of Jupiter

When Jupiter transits **through the Lagna,** this would be a good period to get favour from people around, in both personal and professional matters. This would be an optimistic and positive time. The person would generally get good food which could result in weight gain. There would be expansion in social circle and acquaintances which will be to the person's advantage. There could be chance to mingle with the rich and famous people and those in authority. The person should avoid arrogance to get gains and comfort. Domestic life would be happier. There could be travels with respect to profession or business. When Jupiter is afflicted in natal chart as well as during its transit in the Lagna indications could be contrary to what explained above.

Sextile to a House: When Jupiter transits sextile to a house, that is when it is 60° away from a house, it has sextile aspect on the house. This would be a fortunate period for social contacts, and the person will gain from them. Group working will be beneficial rather than working alone. There could be some gains through friends, co-workers and neighbours etc. Chance of working on good projects would be there. Should try and expand one's contacts with larger world, many people could become permanent friends to one's advantage. Existing friends will be helpful, partnership with them will go well and profitable and helpful to others.

Square to a House: When Jupiter transits a Square or Kendra to a house that is at 90° to a house under consideration, there would good relations with everyone with some minor pitfalls. This would be a period of growth through contacts with others, and one should avoid acting with arrogance so as not to annoy others which could hamper their progress. There would be some fortunate opportunity during this period which indicates some chance to work through a friend or associate and get good gains. Generally people would help in personal and professional matters as well giving peace of mind. Negotiations and transactions would be good, provided one pays attention to the details.

Trine to a House: When Jupiter transits Trine or Kona to a house that is at 120° to a house under consideration, this would be a period of growth and expansion through the individual's contacts, relations and friends and the experiences he/she gets to go through. The person would be more helpful and optimistic and will be helped in return. Spiritual tendencies will grow during this period. This would be a time of beginning of great emotional happiness, relations, may be new love, which could be beneficial and last long and will be of help to the personal growth.

Opposite to a House: When Jupiter transits a house opposite to the one under consideration that is the seventh house from a house under consideration, this period is important to be careful and the individual should not be selfish and his/her behaviour and approach should be calibrated especially for advancing once career. Some individual could come into one's life who would be of much help in some way that is either through partnership, love relations or marriages etc. which will be beneficial to the person. He/she may be attracted romantically to someone who will be important to them. If there is any case in court of law, this would be a good time to consult a lawyer. There would be domestic peace and harmony. This transit of Jupiter is quite good for conjugal happiness, partnership businesses, solemnising marriage etc. Any marital or family issues affecting a love relationship may get resolved with some initiatives and efforts during this period.

Transit of Saturn

When Saturn transits through the Lagna, it is one of the most significant transit of life. The responsibilities would increase considerably so the individual should work hard and systematically, to complete them gracefully. There could be less freedom of movement than usual, high pressure of work would be there, some old tasks left unfinished could get done with some additional efforts. Superiors could burden the individual with more responsibility which would turn out productive rather than disruptive. The person should avoid taking up or initiating new projects as there could be difficulties ahead, thus it is advisable to complete the old projects, work load etc.

Good relations may not suffer whereas bad ones could become isolated. Focus should be on maintaining and developing good relations with people who matter. Despite difficulties, the person would have a productive time. One will learn worldly tricks and cleverness. There could be some spending on unwanted ventures. If afflicted by a malefic aspect, may lead to seclusion. The individual would generally be successful during this period only after some struggle.

Sextile to a House: When Saturn transits sextile to a house that is when it is 60° away from a house, it has sextile aspect on the house and Saturn has a special sextile aspect. The individual needs to take this transit seriously and it is important to set a disciplined course and order to the duties because the pattern that one establishes during this period would be difficult to change, thus it is better to set a disciplined order and punctuality in one's life which could determine the success or failures of the duties and relations over the next several years. One should keenly gauge and listen to others' viewpoint, and should not believe them on the face value, neither should they be rejected outright. Older people could be helpful. Being worried or with occupied mind one may prefer serious work and company of serious people.

Square to a House: When Saturn transits a Square or Kendra to a house that is at 90° to a house under consideration, this would be a time of severe testing in your relations with others. The individual needs to re-evaluate all his/her relations with a holistic view weighing all the pros and cons. Some people who have close relations with the person may support in critical situations. The person may feel alone and out of touch with everyone out there and may feel that he/she has no support from anyone, even their loved ones.

Trine to a House: When Saturn transits Trine or Kona to a house that is at 120° to a house under consideration, during this period the individual's actions and behaviour will maintain an equilibrium which will become reliable and consistent. His/her approach to problems will be disciplined, well-ordered and matured and they may find difficulties to changes, so they need to be flexible for the solution of the problems. A good period for self-sufficiency and getting help from others. One should be cautious in forming new relationships, older people will be more beneficial. Someone from any part of their life could enter into the affairs to help and that individual could remain unknown.

Opposite to a House: When Saturn transits a house opposite to the one under consideration that is the seventh house from a house under consideration, strains and tensions in relations with life partner or business partner could take place which may result in separation or strained relationships, however these can be overcome by truthful and transparent communication from all the parties involved. Fear, anxiety and some losses through opponents or critics could have a significant break-through in the life of the individual. The past efforts and work started in his/her profession could get completed during this period. This period would be quite critical time, when the person should work carefully and has to safeguard his/her health as well. As far as possible it would be better to avoid shortcuts for success, otherwise plans could get delayed.

Chapter 6

Retrogression of Planets

Transits or the current planetary position and their movement in space is the reason for retrogression. Planets from the point of view of the earth will appear to slow down and apparently be stationary. Then they appear to move backward, due to the faster speed of earth, this motion is known as retrograde motion of the planets. This apparent retrograde movement is due to the motion of the earth's orbit. The Sun and the Moon never retrograde. Rahu Ketu always move in retrograde motion. Retrograde planets in the natal chart or ephemeris are marked by R. Mars R or Jupiter R indicate that these planets were retrograde at the time of consideration for the chart.

Saturn retrogrades for 140 days and remains apparently stationary 5 days before and after. Jupiter retrogrades 120 days and is apparently stationary 5 days before and after. Mars retrogrades for 80 days and is apparently stationary 3 to 4 days before and after. Venus is retrograde for 42 days and is apparently stationary approximately two days before and after. Mercury retrogrades for 24 days and is apparently stationary one day before and after.

Each planet has its own percentage of time when it appears to be retrograde. They are Saturn at 36.39%, Jupiter at 30.24%, Mercury at 19.76%, Mars at 9.33% and Venus at 7.22%.

The Sanskrit name for retrograde planets is known as 'Vakriya'. The potential of the retrograde planets is to be flexible, to twist thing around, to make them unclear, to teach or convey its message in an indirect way, to view life in a different way. The individual can deal with the quality of their retrograde planets in a positive manner or can use their potential in a totally negative way. The indications would be there to do good or bad deeds as per the functional status of the planet but it is up to the individual to use this in the right way.

Rahu Ketu are forever moving backwards and this has led to them being described negatively in the classics. But they also have the potential to view everything in a complete different manner and therefore can be quite innovative and make individual reach heights that they never thought they would conquer, by going against the grain.

The five planets Mars, Mercury, Jupiter, Venus and Saturn express the practical reality of our life. They are the planets that form the Pancha Mahapurusha Yogas that bestows greatness on earth. They rule the Pancha Mahabhutas, the five primary elements that influence our physical body but also sheath the eternal consciousness. These elements control our organs of desires, emotions and senses. They can keep us grounded in gross reality but if we start to use their energy spiritually they become infused with a different power.

All planets and more so the retrograde planets influence the primary structure of the human consciousness and its relationship with its human life. By blocking the chakras and then interfering with the Pancha Mahabhutas, they create disconnection and imbalances, inability to control the senses. An individual has to understand their retrograde planets and nurture certain qualities and traits to bring back the harmony.

Vedic Astrology classics say that retrograde planets are strong. The quality of the planet changes when it turns retrograde. Retrograde planets are closest to earth; therefore their impact on the individual is the strongest. Strong to do what? Two influences of retrograde planets need to be taken into account – their affect in the natal chart and by transit. The individual with retrograde planets does not always know how to control its energy. Therefore they struggle to express the planets qualities - over-emphasizing them or being in denial of their positive or negative qualities or misusing their power. Knowing how to deal with the retrograde in the natal chart is the key. Retrogrades by transit can influence everyone whether we have them in our chart or not. A straight thinking person can suddenly change their ways under the influence of retrograde Mercury. So we all have to learn to cope with the retrograde transit and be aware of them annually.

A planet when debilitated is less potent and powerful (not negative) and thus when it gets retrograde its functionality changes according to its status in the chart, that is if it is a malefic and debilitated and retrograde its maleficence gets reduced and if it is benefic, its beneficence also gets reduced. Similarly an exalted planets is quite potent and powerful (not positive), and if it gets retrograde, if it is functionally malefic its maleficence increases and if it is benefic its beneficence also increases.

Whenever a planet starts in a motion other than the normal course, it yields unusual effects as well. In general, the fields ruled by these planets suffer the major influence. For example, communication hazards would be more during Mercury retrograde. Accidents due to rashness or negligence could take place during Mars retrograde and so on. Hence, each planetary retrogression should be considered as a time to be cautious, and to consider things from a different viewpoint.

Mercury Retrogression

Mercury retrograde promotes either a person talking too much or not at all. Mercury is the karaka of speech, memory, analytical ability and intellect. Their thinking can also could be different during retrogression. They may be very bright thinkers, but not know how to express that or drive others crazy with their ideas, thinking they are the only ones who are the intelligent ones. Mercury's combustion can create more problems. Mercury travels close to the Sun and it is most likely to be combust. Combust and retrograde can make a person very prone to burn out and also unsure of how to deal with themselves during those times, not an easy situation to be in. Mercury rules the Prithvi (Earth) Bhuta(Element). Prithvi deals with being practical and stable. Prithvi also controls the Muladhara chakra. Mercury retrograde can make someone impractical and they are more likely to make their position unstable than those whose Mercury is direct. Retrograde Mercury would show some blocks to the Muladhara chakra.

When Mercury goes retrograde, many of our everyday affairs ruled by Mercury could get disrupted. When Mercury is retrograde, mental mistakes could happen abound inadvertently. Travel plans could get often messed up. Misunderstandings with those in the family or at work can take place. Those who have belief in Vedic Astrology may refrain from making any sort of contract when Mercury is retrograde.

Mercury is the planet that rules communication and thinking. Mercury goes in retrograde motion about three times a year for three weeks of time period each approximately. Whenever this phenomenon takes place, all lines of communication seems to go haywire. Things are misunderstood and information is misapplied. Thinking (in general) leaves the course of "normal". Although some brilliant projects may be sketched out during this period, chances are that more people suffer from anxiety and nervous breakdown at this time. While the planet is Vakriya or retrograde, it is often advised to not to sign any contracts, to look before putting an idea in action, even if it means a verbal commitment. Individual should not rely on every information passing through. Think, watch, analyse because the information presented in front of him/her might be a false one if not totally unnecessary. It is time to process all the learning acquired till now to take decisions.

If Mercury is retrograde in the horoscope itself, it can indicate mental sufferings and anxieties and in the case, if it's negatively placed. If Mercury is well placed, it bestows a brilliant mind. Whatever the case, the result is not `usual`. All the aspects have to be taken in consideration before deriving any conclusion. But most of all, it can also be said that, cashing on the negative or positive influence of the planet is much dependent on a person's Free will. An individual with well-placed Mercury

- Generally reconsiders before speaking
- Have lots of inner conversation and thoughts
- Expresses self, better in writing
- Feels misunderstood

Mercury involves mental processes and communication of all kinds. Exploring ideas, seeking knowledge, writing, public speaking, making contacts, even short trips and commerce fall into Mercury's domain. Mercury is retrograde at least three times each year, and is our most frequently retrograde planet. During this usually three week timeframe, misunderstandings increase, mail and email gets lost, messages may delayed or appear elsewhere, misdirection and frustration with miscommunications of all kinds tend to intensify. Odd ideas tend to occur as normal abilities and patterns of writing, learning, and speech could become disrupted.

For a few, this retrograde actually has the opposite effect. New ideas, new speaking or writing abilities are often revealed in folks whose natal Mercury is retrograde. If an individual is normally hesitant or afraid to speak out, or if finds himself/herself very concerned with how others will take their words or what would happen if they speak their mind. Those few, may tend to get a kind of vacation from or improvements in both their usual internal and external dialogue.

In Karmic terms, Mercury retrograde in an individual's natal chart suggests that he/she may be dealing with old lessons about the negative consequences of uninhibited speech. Motives could mean a lot to them and could find themselves attracting more than their share of criticism or opposition to their ideas, but if they let that stop themselves from speaking their mind, they would be essentially inhibiting themselves from communicating. They need to learn to overcome fears. Most other people are actually more concerned with how the world sees them than they are about what they think about the individual. The individual should apply curiosity, flexibility, and take an active interest in the welfare or interests of people around themselves. Half of their ability would come from listening. If speaking to groups of people makes them nervous, then they should let their thoughts escape into the outside world by writing. Attempts should be made to make small talk wherever possible about any topics of interest, which would boost the self-confidence and begin to overcome their hesitance of expounding their personal views in public.

Venus Retrogression

Venus is the Karaka for all the good and positive things in life, comforts, luxuries, marriage, sexual pleasures, wealth etc. It being retrograde does makes the person choose unusual alliances. The individual may have an unconventional view of others or when in marriage or relationship do not know how to express their love and/or feelings well. Venus also deals with femininity, and women with Venus retrograde do not always understand how to be truly feminine. They can become overtly masculine or forget to dress feminine and be feminine. People with retrograde Venus may want something different from their relationships and their concept of the women/men in their life is different. Venus rules

Apas Bhuta, the water element. The human body is composed of over 85% water. Water deals with emotions, taste, happiness and peace. Retrograde Venus can create problems with all these.

The effect of Venus retrograde can be disastrous/miraculous to a happy married life, with of course, depending on its position in the chart being of paramount importance. As Venus slowly turns retrograde, the person could gradually gets disinterested in sexual activities, could be other way also depending on its position in Chart, Timing, Transit etc. Venus seems to work alike in all signs when retrograde. It affects individuals in many ways than normally understood.

Venus retrogression is related to luxuries in life, as well as relationships with near and dear ones. If the transit of Venus is in retrograde motion, one should be thoughtful about all the relationships they are living, and the way they relate to others. It is also the time the individual should reconsider their material gains in life. The extent or type of influence of Venus retrogression depends upon its position in the charts. But nevertheless, it is the time to be watchful, as it is a period for strong emotional ups and downs.

If Venus is retrograde in the natal chart, it can indicate emotional and material difficulties (in case it is badly placed). If it is well placed, it indicates extreme emotional attractions and repulsions. The result will always be a far cry from normal. A person with retrograde Venus would generally show the following tendencies, particularly if the placement in Chart is not conducive.

a) Reconsiders before expressing love or affection
b) Relates awkwardly to others
c) Doubts the love others offer
d) Can become obsessed in relationships
e) Feels let down by the commitment level of others

Venus involves pleasure, love, romance, relaxation, aesthetics, peaceful feelings, harmony, money, and values. Venus tends to work by attraction. Approximately every eighteen months or so, Venus slips into retrograde for about six weeks approximately. While Venus is retrograde, the individual is more likely to find his/her ability to attract what they want restricted or inhibited, conversely it can/may increase as well depending on the placement in the chart. The person could find himself/herself much more concerned with achieving or maintaining external beauty, flow of ready cash, questioning their ideas of pleasure, aesthetics, or even revaluating their feelings about romantic relationships.

A natal Venus retrograde can indicate you difficulty achieving fulfilment or finding the right romantic partner. They may be more in love with their ideas about love than they are with any real person they know. In Karmic terms, one need to complete a life lesson about giving and receiving love and affection. The person is here to determine what is truly of value to themselves and learn about creating a balance of give and take in their life. Their romantic dialogue has a tendency to be far too internal at times, causing them to inhibit the flow of good things into their life. They need to be willing to experience loving and being loved in order to attract what they desire into their life and create the feelings of security they need.

Mars Retrogression

Mars retrogrades once in two years. Retrograde Mars in natal chart can bring out power issues, how to deal with conflict and aggression and anger. As Mars also represents muscular energy amongst many others, its retrogression can create problems with how you deal with the energy within. It is often seen in charts of individuals who have problems with their sexuality- they can be overtly aggressive or completely suppress their masculine side whereby creating imbalance in personality. Individuals have to watch they do not become too aggressive and angry. As Mars is about power, its retrogressions give a lot of power yet the individual may not understand their own power and how to use it properly. This can lead to its misuse. Mars rules Agni Bhuta of Fire element so its retrogression can create too much fire or complete exhaustion. They have to watch their metabolism. It can get speeded up or be totally dull. The chakra is Manipura, which deal with balance, vision and energy. Retrograde Mars tends to block the way this chakra works and create problems on a subtle level. Mars also deals with logic and here the logic can get skewered or twisted. It can also make a person whose logic is unconventional but at the same time very powerful and they can reach places where others cannot as they have the ability to see things from backward to forward.

Mars retrograde in a person's birth chart indicates, the person to be very frigid or could go to the extremes. Some have sex aversions. During its slow moving period, two weeks before and after retrogression it starts to indicate its effects. Retrogression of Mars is a high time to control and channelise the individual's energy and drive, and prevent it from getting out of hand. One has to be thoughtful about their actions and cautious about getting rash and scattered. It's the right time to reconsider the agenda on hand, and to be firmly rooted in ground reality. It is also the time to reenergize, rather than burning energies in fruitless pursuits.

If Mars is Retrograde in the horoscope itself, the person can be accident prone, or inclined to illness, in case of a wrongly placed Mars. If the Mars is well placed, the individual has an unusual way of handling his/her affairs and actions. Whatever the case, effects are far from normal. Again its dependent on an individual's own free will to control the final outcome.

Mars retrogression indicates, the individual

- Reconsiders before expressing anger
- Finds competitive situations hard to handle
- Tends to suppress things
- Can become depressed

Mars represents direct energy, physical expression, individual action and assertiveness, as well as anger, desire, sexuality, competitiveness and motivation for self-interest. Mars energies tend to burst forward exerted in short duration. Every two years Mars goes retrograde for approximately over two months. What often results are, upsets and frustrations in daily life as emotions which should be externalized becoming internalized, a kind of chewing up one's self. When one finally tends to open up, it is likely, as not that in doing so you will be acting out aggressively against you're their self-interest.

If one has Mars in retrograde in their natal chart, they may find that, they are waging an internal battle causing difficulty in asserting themselves because they could be afraid of the consequences of releasing their emotions. The person may tend to over think before he/she acts and may find that they have a tendency to hold back. In Karmic terms, they are likely to be attempting to make up for some vaguely recollected but deeply influential past misdeeds which they may now regret. Whatever the cause, they are holding themselves back instead of standing up directly for their own interests. This works directly against the life lesson which they are here to accomplish. The individual would be learning about themselves, defining who they are by what actions they take. They will need to let go of timidity or a lack of direction in order work out how they can initiate actions without creating a chaos of needless destruction.

Jupiter Retrogression

Jupiter is the guru or the teacher. An individual with Jupiter retrograde usually never knows when to stop giving advice. They can be very knowledgeable yet they do not know how to use this knowledge in the right way. They can also mistrust their own wisdom. On a positive level they can have a look at issues with a very different viewpoint. They will also give advice that is unconventional and different. As Jupiter is the Karaka of children, it can show children who are different. Jupiter as a Karaka of husbands in a female chart will indicate a husband who is different. On an extreme negative level, they can bring twisted thinking into the relationship. Jupiter rules the Aakash Bhuta or Space element. Space deals with the knowledge, wisdom, ability to purify, to repel the negative forces. Jupiter being retrograde weakens the ability to use this Tatva. Vishuddhi chakra could become blocked and this make us feel unprotected and make some wrong choices. Vishuddhi also purifies the poisons, here the poisons of the mind do not always get the right filter. So the person does not know how to stop them from polluting the life.

When this planet of growth and expansion is in retrogression, a lot many projects that were due for expansion and launch may get delayed, or stop altogether. This is the time when a person needs to think about his/her own inner resources, and use that knowledge to get the work done. Most probably, the person might come up with the conclusion that the stopped work was actually not necessary, and there are other better resources available. This is the ideal time for individuals to `expand` within themselves. Individuals with retrograde Jupiter, often get success in other people's failures. They have the unique ability to succeed in projects that were abandoned by others. Such people revive sick companies and uncover hidden assets. In order to achieve their mental goal they prefer to bargain.

When Jupiter is retrograde in the natal chart, either it makes the person too fickle or vain (if badly placed). Or it gives unusual heights of knowledge and wisdom to the native. Also Jupiter retrograde

- has doubts about what they deserve and so ...
- finds it easy to settle for crumbs
- feels superior in some way inside
- abundance is felt on the inside
- looks inside for answers to religious questions

Jupiter represents the principles of expansion, gambling, speculation, luck, opportunities, optimism, abundance, travel, higher education, teaching, religion and philosophy. Approximately four months a year, this planet slips into retrograde. When it does, the individual is likely to see its influence roll through one's life and society around themselves. Plans have a tendency to implode. Jupiter retrograde influences individuals internally to look within to seek new meanings. One may find that they can best use these opportunities to revaluate their life and reach new levels of awareness and understanding.

If Jupiter is retrograde in the natal chart, the person have a very rich internal life. They actually make their own luck. Abundance is felt within as they search the world looking to discover truth and develop a broader philosophy of life and living. At the same time, they may feel hesitant about involving themselves too deeply in others affairs or sharing their views out of a concern for being thought so different that they may be cast out by public opinion. Speculations may not bring them all the external rewards they seek, but each time they take a chance, their adventures allow them to gain from a wide variety of experiences. They must remain open and honest with themselves in order to expand their spirituality and allow their inner voice to guide them.

Saturn Retrogression

Saturn retrograde usually do not know when to stop working. Or they may not like work at all. As Saturn is the Karaka of misery, it is important that one must not give into a negative attitude to life and embrace depression as a habit. Saturn is usually depicted as the planet indicating poor life. The poor are usually hungry - for food, for material goods, for good things in life. Saturn retrogression can make individuals hungry with desire, wanting more and more even when if the hunger has been appeased and they may be materially very well off. They need to watch for greed. Saturn rules Vayu Bhuta or Air element. Vayu is air and Vayu needs to be used constructively otherwise it can become unnecessarily be destructive. Retrogrades do not know how to use their energy so if they do not take care, Saturn can become destructive force for them. Anahata chakra as mentioned in all Vedas and Scriptures teach dispassion and detachment. When this chakra is blocked by retrogression then they can find it difficult to detach.

This retrogression period can cause unexpected delays and interruptions. Obstacles un-thought can spring up taking your priority. The period usually lasts for 4 and half months, during which many feel frustrated and unable to handle hurdles. This is the right time to sit back and reconsider all that one is doing. It is not a proper time to make new starts, but rather learn from the failures in the past and the ones in hand. In individual horoscope, the house that occupied by Saturn will see the effect of retrogression, i.e. that aspect of the life will get affected, along with the general benefic/malefic effect.

Persons with Saturn Retrograde in their birth charts do not like to be known in public, they find security in intellectuals or spirituals. They easily yield to external influences. They appear shy, uneasy, introvert, lacking in self assertion or attempt to cover their lapse with the pretext of arrogance. They feel alone, isolated, separated from their friends and are seldom understood and very reserved. Individuals with retrograde Saturn

- Feel they're never good enough inside
- Indulgent outward behaviour may mask inner feelings of inadequacy
- Hides fears

Saturn deals with Karma, limits, responsibility, tradition, conservatives, authorities, long term goals and accomplishments patiently created, taking responsibility, creating structure, and setting boundaries. Once a year the planet Saturn goes into retrograde for about four-and-a-half months. During this influence, the individual will probably find it unwise to attempt sudden changes or to rush through things. Take practical steps and accept limitations while one takes serious steps toward his/her long term goals. Saturn retrograde can cause one to become their own hardest taskmaster, limit their actions or leave them feeling blocked and pessimistic. .

Saturn retrograde in one's natal chart, indicates that they are likely to have been abused by those with power over you, perhaps having faced unfair situations at home. The person may need to declare personal boundaries, to work out conflicts with authority on a Karmic scale. One could feel that fate conspires against their desires but it's really the individual who is putting the brakes on through feelings of persecution or inhibition in the house where it is placed until they work out how to face doing or confronting whoever or whatever it is that threatens them. Their lesson is one of patience and steady application of hard work as they overcome the impatient urge to cut corners. Everything they gain will be hard won but they will eventually succeed, win the respect of others and actually can shine where they faced difficulties before.

Retrogrades and Stationary Motions

Even if the individual does not have natal planets in retrograde, he/she can experience them during their retrograde transit. They can temporarily block the elements and create problems in the subconscious if we are not aware of them. The two most difficult retrogrades are Mercury and Saturn. Mercury as it happens so often and Saturn as it can transit over one point of the chart again and again; and create lots of issues. It is important to know retrogression of planets in a given year. The retrograde motion of the running Dasha ruler can change the direction of events. Retrogrades indicate a concentration of energy in the part of the zodiac where they are active. If one has planets in that area then they will have major impact. Retrogrades make life appear to be stuck in limbo, neither moving forward or backward. Saturn and Jupiter retrograde once a year and Mars and Venus one every two years. Mercury retrogrades at least three times a year.

Always be aware of Mercury retrograde. They are stress points in the year. Mercury retrograde creates communication problems and makes life uncomfortable. Stress, arguments, delayed journeys - all can make life troublesome during the Mercury retrograde. So do problems with computers, internet, and other technologies. Double check all appointments, travel programmes and journeys- remember not to stop one's life. Decisions made during Mercury retrograde can be changed after it goes direct.

Special care and attention needs to be given when planets retrograde over the Gandanta points. Gandanta points are the junctions of Rashis or Signs pertaining to Fire and Water elements. The Gandanta points are first 3° 20' of Mesha or Aries representing Ashwini Nakshatra's 1st Charan(part), last 3° 20' of Meena or Pisces representing Revati Nakshatra's 4th Charan(part); last 3° 20' of Karka or Cancer represented by Aslesha Nakshatra's 4th Charan(part) and first 3° 20' of Simha or Leo represented by Makha Nakshatra's 1st Charan(part); last 3° 20' of Vrischika or Scorpio represented by Jyeshtha Nakshatra's 4th Charan(part) and first 3° 20' of Dhanu or Sagittarius represented by Moola Nakshatra's 1st Charan(part). Retrogression within these points is generally indicated (depending on the chart), by instabilities, upheavals, financial turmoils, some major changes in national or world orders etc.

The stationary points of Saturn, before and after retrogression is quite important. If a natal planet is on the same degree as Saturn stations during its transit, then one can expect that to be a major issue to contend with. This becomes even more important during difficult Saturn transits like Sade Sati, which is itself a troublesome transit, of course depending on the chart, as Sadesati would be quite productive for some ascendants. Saturn stationing over the exact degree of the Moon will bring mental stress and in some cases accidents and injuries. The house ruler-ship and placement of the Moon would indicate where the problem could be. Also Saturn can transit over the same point for longer duration, which concentrates the energy of its difficult influence.

The stationary points of Jupiter are also important. This can positively enhance good qualities. It can make people think in wrong ways. Or encourage the possibility of getting wrong advice. Traditionally in India, marriage, auspicious events and new ventures are not planned when Jupiter is retrograde, but this approach is not correct for all and individual charts should be analysed in particular to plan events.

The stationary points of Mars: This can lead to war or aggressive tendencies. Mars retrograde can increase stubbornness and can herald a time for conflicts.

In practice, retrograde planets generally seem to affect the mental plane more than the physical or worldly plane. Those with retrograde planets often respond to 'time' in a nonstandard way. Retrogression could represent an intrinsic strength in ones being or may represent an armour with cracks in it, the outcome depending upon how well the retrograde planet is connected with other factors in the chart.

Chapter 7

Transit of Jupiter

Jupiter transits through a Rashi or Sign in approximately one year. The transits are analysed with respect to natal Moon position however they can also be analysed from the natal ascendant.

Jupiter Transits the First House

When Jupiter transits the first house, the person feels optimistic, cheerful, and content and may receive tributes, promotions, gifts, and courtesies. People generally behave kindly to the person, and his/her relationships are pleasant and fruitful. Desires get accomplished with little resistance, and the person generally succeeds. It is an excellent time to approach powerful or influential individuals. If the person has been seeking a pay raise or advancement at work, he/she may now attain that goal. Opportunities continually arise and the individual should take advantage of them.

His/her faith in God would become stronger during this time and may enjoy a special sense of appreciation. His/her religious, spiritual, and devotional tendencies could increase and may get favoured by gurus, mentors, or teachers of philosophy and higher knowledge. He/she gains any knowledge, education, and wisdom they seek. It is a good time for self-improvement and all kinds of growth. If the person deals with the public in any way, he/she may now become better known or even famous. His/her confidence and enthusiasm would be infectious. People would get attracted to happy spirit, and the leadership qualities may get fine-tuned. In competition, the person has better chance to win against peers and associates.

Individuals who are particularly jovial to begin with, gain tremendous abundance and fortune during this time with some exceptions depending the natal chart. However, such individuals must be careful not to indulge in excessive pleasure and diversions. They must beware of conceit, egotism, or becoming carried away with their own infallibility. The person may gain weight bringing in some health issues later, when Jupiter transits the first house. In the exuding optimism, the person expands his/her activities as well as the sphere of influence. They may begin many new endeavours that have an excellent chance of success. There may be interest in travel, law, and philosophy. The person enjoys friendships, as he/she would be the focus of everyone's attention and goodwill. There is more joy, contentment, fun, and serenity in their life. He/she feels secure and gains in honour and prestige. Investments and speculations could produce good results, and the person benefits from whatever risks taken. When Jupiter transits the first house, it aspects the fifth, seventh and the ninth house. The aspect to the fifth means the person experiences great creativity and mental harmony. Relationships with children are favoured, and conception of a child is possible. Jupiter's seventh house aspect indicates the possibility of marriage or an important new love relationship. The aspect to the ninth house signifies travel, auspicious religious experiences, attainment of higher knowledge, and good luck.

Jupiter Transits the Second House

When a functionally benefic Jupiter transits the second house, the person experiences a joyful sense of abundance and worthiness, if in the case the Jupiter is functionally malefic some opposing results could get indicated. The person would generally attract significant financial gains and material possessions, may discover resources wherever they are to be found. It is a happy period in which the person feels, is getting tangible benefits as a result of his/her own virtue. If the person is not materially oriented, then instead of acquiring money, may create rewards that are appropriate to the value system. During the previous Jupiter transit (of the first house), the person received praise, accolades, favouritism, and luck in general. In this transit the person gets to experience the blessings that the physical universe has to offer, in their most basic form. The person feels secure, protected, and cared for. He/she is not plagued by feelings of scarcity or doubt and feels good about themselves and expects to receive their due. All money matters are favoured, and the person profits from business dealings, speculations, and occupational investments. He/she may receive pay raises, pending payments, stipends, or other monetary benefits.

The second house governs family life, education, knowledge, and writing, in addition to wealth. Therefore, the person may enjoy happy domestic life and expands his/her relationships. May begin new studies or return to school. Or he may decide to give out knowledge through teaching or writing. It is an excellent time for those in literary or intellectual professions. As Jupiter transits the second house, it simultaneously aspects the sixth, eighth, and tenth houses.

The favourable aspects to the sixth and tenth houses mean the person succeeds easily in his work and career. The aspect to the eighth house brings wealth through partnerships and joint finances. If Jupiter is functionally malefic the positive indications could get toned down. The person may borrow money with little restrictions or difficulties.

Jupiter Transits the Third House

The third house is said to govern courage, adventures, energy, and the fulfilment of daily desires, as well as publications, friendships, communication and siblings. The person now could fulfil his/her daily desires with ease and would be able to run errands all day long without getting tired or meeting with frustrations and delays. May accomplish his/her objectives, meets the goals, and still has energy left over. It is a time of incessant activity wherein the person pursues his/her interests and promotes his endeavours powerfully and effectively. He/she could enjoy many adventures.

The person would be energetic and active within immediate surroundings, and relationships with siblings and relatives are favoured. The person may enjoy the company of his brothers and sisters, or receive benefits, blessings, and advantages from them. He/she would constantly could undergo short journeys. Interacts more with friends, neighbours, and relatives than usual. The third house also rules the fine arts, music, dance, singing, and drama. He/she could get involved in these and may enjoy these fields and may professionally progress if he/she has undertaken these as a profession.

As Jupiter transits the third house, it simultaneously aspects the seventh, ninth, and eleven houses. The aspect to the seventh house indicates the possibility of marriage or a significant new love relationship, if Jupiter is functionally benefic. The ninth house aspect signifies good luck, long-distance travel, and favourable experiences. Jupiter's aspect on the eleventh house means positive group activity and good rapport with friends. It also indicates benefits from the eldest sibling and financial gains from "side ventures" other than one's daily means of support.

Jupiter Transits the Fourth House

When a benefic Jupiter transits the fourth house, domestic life is favoured. The person locates surroundings perfectly suited to his/her needs and feels a sense of balance and stability. He/she is likely to move to a new apartment, house, or city. Nature supports his/her endeavours and the person may find exactly what they want at an affordable price. Even if the person does not intend to live on the acquired land, will gain from real estate investments. The person may refurnish his/her residence, or make other renovations and home improvements. He/she would obtain great pleasure from landscaping, gardening, farming, or any hobby involving the earth and may also feel strong emotional attachments to their material belongings.

The fourth house represents happiness, heart, conveyances, education and comforts as well as land and homes. Therefore, during Jupiter's fourth house transit the person would be happy and content, and successful in obtaining some of the above. When Jupiter transits the fourth, it simultaneously aspects the eighth, tenth, and twelfth houses. The aspects to the eighth and twelfth houses bring interest in astrology, metaphysical studies, and spiritual growth. The eighth house aspect also signifies good results with wills, legacies, joint finances, and money from "unearned" sources that is lotteries, insurance benefits, etc. The twelfth house aspect gives the possibility of travel to foreign countries, along with beneficial experiences in such lands.

Jupiter's glance on the tenth house means career success and expansion of one's influence in the professional sphere.

The person could become interested in long-term security and ensuring the well-being of the family. May feel safer and more protected than ever in own habitat and optimistically begin to build a base for the future, from a position of abundance. May focus on collectibles, possessions, property, or any fixed assets which help provide future security. He/she would feel strong and enjoy inner peace. He/she has a sense of belonging and would be happy and secure within familial traditions. Enjoys wonderful social gatherings at home.

Jupiter Transits the Fifth House

The fifth house rules kingship, the mind, mantras, and past-life credit, memory, intelligence, higher education, children, good credits, honours and awards etc. Therefore, the person is mentally happy and spirited. During a benefic Jupiter's transit through the fifth house. The individual could be interested in Holy Scriptures, mantras or other spiritual techniques. He/she will sense the destiny and purpose of their existence and realize what they deserve, for better or for worse. When Jupiter transits the fifth house, it simultaneously aspects the ninth, eleventh, and first houses. The aspects to the first and ninth houses indicate good luck and favouritism. There will also be general good health and well-being, as well as ninth house benefits of travel, higher knowledge, and blessings from elders and spiritual teachers. The favourable aspect to the eleventh house means good results with groups, friends, and the siblings. The person has an easy time fulfilling major goals and desires, and opportunities are consistent and abundant.

When a benefic Jupiter transits the fifth house, artistic endeavours are favoured. The person is creative, imaginative, original in behaviour, and self-expressive. If the person is an artist by profession, he/she is likely to experience one of their most significant and prolific years. The person welcomes pleasure, joy, and fun into life as never before. He/she would enjoy romance for the sheer infatuation, excitement and passion of it and may get in to a love affair.
They also gain great pleasure from sports or competitive activities.

All activities involving children are favoured, including a strong possibility of pregnancy or childbirth. This transit is quite gratifying and fortunate for teachers and parents. The person enjoys a year of happiness, popularity, and individual purpose. He/she would be optimistic about taking risks, and is confident that all will be well no matter what the outcome. They would feel powerful in their individuality and strong in ego. They function from a position of abundance, and, as a result, their social interactions would be successful. They would feel a healthy sense of self-love and dignity. Their will power would be strong during this period and he may feel comfortable about the possibility of leadership, fame, or recognition.
Speculations are favoured, and the person could do well in gambling, stocks, or investment

undertakings, depending on the strength of fifth house in the natal chart.

Jupiter Transits the Sixth House

The sixth house indicates health, wellness, enemies, competitors, litigations and legal issues, service and/or business, problems in marriage or partnerships etc. When a benefic Jupiter transits the house, the person is not bothered by rivals, opponents, or jealous people. Neither is he/she likely to be accused in legal cases, would be generally maintaining good health. As Jupiter transits the sixth, it simultaneously aspects the tenth, twelfth, and second houses. The favourable aspects to the tenth and second make this a good year for wealth and career expansion. The person also benefits from education, knowledge, or any literary undertakings. He/she succeeds in doing good deeds for society at this time. Jupiter's aspect to the twelfth house means the person is not plagued by unexpected debts and expenses. Growth would be steady, and would make good progress on the spiritual path. Travel to remote and/or foreign places.

When Jupiter transits the sixth house, the person thrives on work, self-improvement, and self-healing. It is a time for personal growth and development of one's particular methods, practices, and routines. The person succeeds in daily job, and their work meets with little resistance or criticism. They enjoy even menial tasks or detail-oriented assignments, technicalities and normally tedious jobs don't bother them. His/her projects and endeavours are stress-free. The person gets along well with co-workers, bosses, and employees. They feel enthusiastic about their job, and working conditions may improve at this time. The person's efficiency and precision grow stronger and may now become more specialized in work. If the person decides to seek new employment, he/she is likely to succeed in his quest.

During this period the person is capable of strengthening his/her body and healing deficiencies or health problems and can obtain good medical care easily. It is a good time to begin a new diet or fitness regimen. However, traditional astrological texts report a strong possibility of gaining weight during this transit. Therefore, the person should be careful not to let overconfidence about his/her health lead to overindulgence in sweets or other cravings.

Jupiter Transits the Seventh House

During this period the person could be diplomatic, and experiences peace and harmony, and a powerful sense of appreciation. Love comes quite naturally to him/her and would be sociable, generous, affectionate, and capable of intimacy. Jupiter transit the seventh house, gives aspect to the eleventh, first, and third houses. The person effortlessly fulfils daily desires and major goals. They would have tremendous energy for daily errands and minor tasks throughout this transit. Relationships with siblings, both younger and older, are favoured, as are friendships and group activities. Jupiter's aspect to the first house means promotions, advancement, good luck, fortune, and a measure of spiritual development. The seventh house represents passions, marital relations, partnerships etc. and therefore the person can expect strong sexual desires and cravings, which may get fulfilled.

When Jupiter transits the seventh house, the person has opportunities for fruitful partnerships and love relationships. His/her happiness comes from sharing life with another person. They attract persons of the opposite sex, and learn much about themselves in the process. They may be attracted to special, wealthy, famous, or spiritual persons may become interested in someone from a foreign country or of a different philosophy or background. It is a time of optimism, enthusiasm, and expansion of one's social boundaries. Relationships initiated at this time generally produce happiness and good fortune. However, it should be noted that for many people this transit coincides with separation, divorce or the ending of a relationship if Jupiter is malefic. If the person has been enduring an abusive or life-damaging relationship with no improvement in sight, then they may realise that they deserve better and begins to see ample opportunities to have their needs met properly. Some individuals involved in difficult partnerships of course may find that their situations improve at this time. His/her consciousness may be raised or expanded as a result. The person may obtain support from wealthy benefactors or philanthropists. In any event, there could be significant fortune, opportunity, and luck in one-on-one associations with others.

Jupiter Transits the Eighth House

When a benefic Jupiter transits the eighth house, it aspects the twelfth, second, and fourth houses. The aspect to the twelfth house means a time of growth, spiritual development, bargains, sexual enjoyment, and the possibility of travel to remote places and foreign countries. The aspect to the second house indicates good luck in earning wealth and favourable learning experiences. The fourth house aspect signifies that the person may move or obtain a new home or new conveyance. He/she would benefit from mother or family, and their relationship would bring happiness at this time.

The person could experience a degree of unity and oneness with the world around him/her. This could be a spiritual transit during which the person would feel connected to people and absorbed in the experience without feeling undue attachment to either. He/she would proceed on the path of liberation, from the usual lifestyle. That is, the happiness and stability do not depend on the success or failure of anything external. The result is a sense of genuine freedom. The person is freed from undue sensitivity and the need to control experience in order to avoid pain or suffering. They feel emotionally resourceful and resilient, open to others, and unafraid to be vulnerable maintain power and dignity while merging their identity and individuality with others, especially loved ones.

Occult and spiritual endeavours would get favoured during this period. The person may visit psychics, astrologers, or anyone who can help him/her uncover secret, hidden knowledge, or they may conduct their own research into metaphysical subjects. As the person would tend to be free from the usual attachments, fears, desires, and complexes, he/she would be able to delve deeply into issues which they might normally feel sensitive about. Thus it would be a good time for healing or transforming afflicted features of the personality. The person may realise death as a natural experience and confront their mortality with a sense of hopefulness. He/she may consider the reality of astral travel, reincarnation, or immortality. Intuition would be strong during this period and the person feels peaceful and serene about such talents.

Jupiter Transits the Ninth House

The ninth house represents luck, good fortune, relation with one's father, foreign travels, spiritual inclination and progress and is considered the best house of the birth chart. Therefore, the person experiences good fortune, happiness, and blessings during this period. They are favoured by their spiritual preceptors and is protected from harm. The ninth house is taken to represent the father as well and a father always protects his children. Therefore, activities involving the father are favoured, and the person could gain benefits from him. When Jupiter transits the ninth house, it aspects the first, third, and fifth houses from there. The aspect to the first house means good health, promotions, favouritism progress in prosperity and general happiness. The third house aspect indicates the ability to fulfil daily desires. Associations with all siblings brings benefits. Jupiter's aspect on the fifth house signifies pregnancy or childbirth, favourable experiences with children, successful investments, and mental exuberance.

When Jupiter transits the ninth house, the person expands his/her boundaries, both literally and philosophically. They explore new religions, ideologies, and paradigms, which broaden their awareness. They learns as much as possible about foreign affairs and previously unfamiliar ways of living. They travels to other cities or countries, where they would be successful and productive in their endeavours.

The person may now engage in consciousness expanding techniques, self-development programs. It is a time of idealism and mental optimism. The person learns about the purpose of existence and the truths of life. He/she perceives life in a macroscopic way and enthusiastically contemplates their faith in God. They do well in writing or publishing. It is an excellent time to write a book or any important literary endeavour. Activities with teachers, mentors, and religious figures are very favoured. Individuals pursuing a spiritual path may enjoy a period of great jubilation, joy, and bliss with their guru or mentor. Spiritual growth is enhanced, as life experience is now augmented by higher knowledge. The effect is integrating, and powerfully enriches the person's sense of judgement, wisdom, and discernment. Because they see the whole picture, hence are better able to measure priorities, fathom consequences, and draw appropriate conclusions. They understand how to balance their intuitive faculties with their logical and reasoning powers. There is an understanding between heart and mind.

The person may do well in business dealings involving import, export or trading. They may also do well with foreign jobs and contracts and would feel inspired and would take their ideals and visions seriously. During this period they may be somewhat prophetic in perceiving the future and would reflect on morals, ethics, and principles, and may involve themselves in noble causes. They could enthusiastically promote freedom or a particular religion or spiritual aspects. They benefit from religious and spiritual ceremonies and rituals.

Jupiter Transits the Tenth House

When Jupiter transits the tenth house it aspects the second, fourth, and sixth houses which makes this an excellent time for financial benefits, good working conditions, and success in all practical matters and worldly affairs. Health would generally remain good and the person would not be bothered by enemies and competitors. Education is favoured and family life prospers. The fourth house aspect means the person is happy and content, also the individual could benefit from his/her mother as their relationship flourishes.

Educational degrees can be obtained during this time. The person may obtain land, homes and Vehicles for conveyance. He/she may also acquire some jewellery, comforts, and the modern toys of exuberance. The combined effect of Jupiter's influence on the tenth and fourth houses indicates religious or spiritual pilgrimages.

When Jupiter transits the tenth house, the person gains in status, reputation, and fame. He/she becomes known for what they do or who they are. It is an excellent time for career advancement, promotions, and expansion of professional activities. The person receives publicity without asking, and he/she should take full advantage of the opportunity to broaden their sphere of influence and may win awards or gain some recognition. Their actions meet with little resistance, and have the respect and support of peers and the public. They would definitely be favoured by authority figures and government officials.

New ventures or careers could flourish at this time, and good rewards come to those who have been working towards realization of specific career achievements. The person would feel confident, a clear sense of purpose, and a positive attitude towards success. The individual would be in touch with the calling of his/her life. Accomplishments achieved during this time are important and of lasting value, to the extent that the person gets identified with his/her career or role in society, they would then feel their life validated. Knowing that they make a tangible difference in the world around them uplifts both their spirit and psyche. There is an element of self-actualization brought about as the person sees a measure of his/her individual purpose come to a fruition.

Their relationship with father would bring joy and happiness, and the person would have a deep sense of appreciation and gratitude for his/her father's love. Their bond is strengthened and the person may receive benefits, gifts, or profits from the father.

With a highly malefic functional Jupiter and further malefic conjunctions and aspects, in fact totally opposing indications could be felt contrary to what is described above, thus the functional nature of Jupiter should be assessed correctly in every case as per the chart in hand.

Jupiter Transits the Eleventh House

The eleventh house governs gains and profits from business, profession and all other sources. Thus, the person may prosper during this transit. He/she also benefits from their siblings and/or friends. When Jupiter transits the eleventh house, it aspects the third, fifth, and seventh houses. The aspects to the third and seventh houses mean the person could have continuous energy to accomplish daily tasks and errands. There is opportunity for marriage or a significant love relationship due to the aspect on the seventh house, which would be more likely if there is no malefic aspect or connection of any other functionally malefic planet. They could fulfil most of their desires during this period. Jupiter's glance to the fifth gives a probable indication of happiness with respect to matters related to children and favourable relationships, or with respect to some sudden gains and recognitions due to the good deeds of previous incarnations. The person may also receive gifts or benefits from his/her children. Investments and speculations could bring rewards, and the person would be in a happy, exuberant mind. He/she would be creative, imaginative, and original.

When Jupiter transits the eleventh house, the person could realise the fulfilment of important goals and ambitions. Whereas Jupiter's transit of the previous house that is the tenth house indicated status and recognition from the outside world, the person during this period would understand the significance of achieving, or having just previously achieved, long-held fundamental desires and aspirations. They would feel deeply satisfied by their successes. If the person has remained true to their ideals over the years, then they would now feel profoundly rewarded. They could finally accomplish the goals which they would have long-yearned and their strongest desired goals which bring them the most happiness.

Opportunities for prosperity and new endeavours would be plenty and the person gets to concentrate on as many different interests and ambitions as he/she desires. They would have good perspective and know exactly what will bring them happiness and what will not. Friendships are more favoured than ever during this time. The person appreciates his/her friends, and enjoys an excellent social life. He/she makes new acquaintances and has continuous opportunities to expand his/her connections and day-to-day company. They may associate with religious, spiritual, or foreign friends as well and may receive gifts, presents, or donations from friends and will benefit and derive pleasure from all types of group activity at this time, indicating fame and recognition socially. The person would have a sense of belonging, and functions well in organizations, associations, fraternities and the community at large and may especially enjoy participation in spiritual or philosophical groups.

This would be a very good time for the individual to contribute and give back to the society whatever he/she can. Their detached intellect and idealism combine to produce a realistic humanitarian vision. They would have good understanding and would be aware of the sensitivities of the society.

Jupiter Transits the Twelfth House

When a benefic Jupiter transits through the twelfth house, means that the person makes good progress on the path to spirituality, enlightenment. He/she may also visit remote foreign countries for either professional or other purposes. They get bargains and incur no unexpected debts and expenses. They enjoy sexual and bed pleasures and generally get good sleep. When Jupiter transits the twelfth, it also aspects the fourth, sixth, and eighth houses. The aspect to the fourth means the possibility of obtaining land, vehicles, conveyances or moving to a new home or apartment. It also indicates benefits and luck with the mother, educational qualifications, and the person may get jewellery, ornaments, and other luxuries. The aspect to the sixth house means the person would generally not bothered by enemies or competitors, and His/her health could remain generally good. He/she would enjoy his/her daily work and gets along well with their superiors and co-workers. A benefic Jupiter's glance to the eighth house symbolizes money from partners, wills, legacies, and other unearned means. The person could get interested in occult studies and psychology related studies.

When Jupiter transits the twelfth house, the person could relinquish his petty concerns in favour of higher consciousness and spiritual integration. The person feels spiritually and psychologically whole. The grip of his/her emotional and mental boundaries begin to loosen, and is less affected by usual fears, complexes, and attachments. It is a time of self-healing, and the person confronts phobias that have intimidated them in the past. They gain insights into problems stemming from childhood or even from previous lifetimes. They have faith in the higher forces of nature and believe that their needs will be met in due course of time, so they do not fret and they are at peace and approach life with a feeling of abundance.

The person has a better understanding of the purpose of life. They understand the evolutionary process and come to know and understand that they are here to purify their soul and perfect their nature. They are less concerned with acquiring and winning, and more concerned with spiritual growth. It is an excellent time for religious happiness and the study of God or other concepts of infinity. Meditation, introspection, and the quest for spiritual liberation are powerfully favoured. The person may wish to retreat to a monastery or an ashram. If they do so, they can expect happy and fruitful results. The person feels selfless, charitable, and magnanimous. They may volunteer for hospital work or other goodwill activities. They may even travel to far off places to help the needy.

The person feels intrinsically connected to the universe and is relieved of his/her sense of separateness. He/she also becomes cognizant of his/her subconscious mind. Because he/she is in touch with nature and his/her own instincts, the person is protected from serious harm. They may uncover secrets and mysteries within themselves and could have deep spiritual experiences during this period. Their intuition would be strong during this period, and the person would be able to comprehend the meaning and symbolism of their dreams. Occult endeavours bring happiness, and the person may perceive spiritual dimensions beyond his/her normal awareness. They would also feel especially inspired by fine arts, crafts and music.

Chapter 8

Transit of Saturn and *Sadesati*

Saturn is the slowest moving planet and thus provides a chance of analysing and synthesising influences in a little more detail than what would be possible with a faster moving planet.

One Navamsha (Ninth division of a sign of 30 Deg) is of 3 Deg 20min, which exactly corresponds to one quarter of the Nakshatra. 108 Navamshas (9×12) for the twelve Rashis/Signs and 108 Nakshatra quarters (27×4), four quarters each for 27 Nakshatras. The Navamsha span is the same as the Nakshatra Pada/Charan (lunar mansion quarters).

Saturn stays in one Navamsha, i.e. a 3 Deg 20 min arc in the skies for approximately 3 months and 10 days as it completes one round around the Sun i.e. 360 Deg zodiac in 30yrs.

As Transits are taken and analysed with reference to natal Moon position, Saturn's transit acquires significance as it is the slowest and as per the Vedic scripts it is connected with mostly negative things and situations of life, but that is not always the case. Saturn transit can lift up an individual very high in life and make them highly prosperous. The Saturn is significant as it teaches and enforces discipline, punctuality, law and order and justice in every sphere of life and more so with the corresponding attributes of the houses it is associated with.

The transit of Saturn around the natal Moon is called *Sadesati.* This cycle of Sadesati of Saturn starts when Saturn in its transit just enters the Rashi/Sign preceding the natal Moon Rashi/Sign. Thus if an individual is born with natal Moon in the sign Simha/Leo, then for this individual the period of Sadesati starts when Saturn in its transit enters the Rashi/Sign Karka/Cancer. Further the cycle of Sadesati extends for seven and half years, that is two and half years in the sign preceding the natal Moon sign, two and half years in the sign of natal Moon and the last two and half years in the sign succeeding the sign of the natal Moon sign, as Saturn transits each sign for two and half years.

Saturn takes 2 ½ years to move through a single sign and the period of Sade-Sati commences when it enters the sign prior to that occupied by natal Moon or when it just enters the twelfth sign from natal Moon. This is with respect to the Transit of Saturn in the Zodiac. From the 12th house it aspects the 2nd house of the chart and hems the ascendant between itself and its ill influence on the 2nd house. Then after a period of 2 ½ years it enters the ascendant and this phase is the central phase of Sade-Sati. Thereafter it enters the second house after 2 ½ years and stays there for 2 ½ years thus completing the 7½ years cycle around the natal Moon.

Transit results of all planets, not only of Saturn are to be judged from the Moon sign as per Vedic Astrology, at the same time other views of transit analysis around ascendant is also prevalent in some sections. The importance of Lagna/ascendant sign cannot be over-emphasised and at the same time the Moon sign is also not less important.

Moon governs the emotional part of the brain. Some actions are impulsive and Moon gets its importance. Even where impulse is not allowed to govern actions it is observed that sentiments, sensitivities generate the action and as such Moon comes into play. This is to say that anything that influences an individual's feelings influences his/her mind or brain and thus the action of the individual takes importance. It is perhaps on this account that Moon sign gets a precedence over ascendant.

The importance of Moon sign and of ascendant cannot be challenged it is a view of many scholars that Sun sign should also be included in the consideration particularly when the effects of Saturn are under judgment. Sun represents our Aatma or Soul. It is this Soul which takes birth and rebirth to fulfil the desires. We can say that Moon is the desire part of the Soul and the ascendant represents the external physical circumstances in which the Soul has to move in the vehicle, the physical body.

The biggest impact of Sade Sati is that it makes a person impassionate, thoughts of losses, dithering nature, unnecessarily start thinking and worrying of some future issues and always with unpleasant thoughts. This is the worst signification of Saturn. But Saturn also does good by showering the blessings of realisation of reality, hard work, truthfulness and legality. Once an individual knows that he/she is under Sade Sati period, they need to control unwanted anxiety and not lose confidence even due to trivial circumstances.

The first cycle of the 2 ½ years stage has chances of separating one from his/her support system that is, family, money, friends because of disputes or job or sickness or accidents. The second or middle cycle of 2 ½ years stage is the most critical stage that leads to actual transformation related to mind, profession, and one's partner, so this stage is most important for everybody where one needs to indulge in lawful and helpful service. The third and last cycle of 2 ½ years stage is replenishing, which means even if something was negative or lost in the first two cycles, one should consider this stage usually good at the end. However, the intensity and impact of Sade Sati at each stage can vary depending on the Dasha, other transits and overall chart position.

It is also true that, it is not Sade Sati that impacts, but it is the Karmas done in the period before Sade Sati whose impacts are shown during this period and in some cases may be *Karmas* of even previous lives. Rather Sade Sati blesses the individual with a period of 7.5 years to introspect make efforts to rectify all wrongs done before Sade Sati.

Saturn has a depressing influence on the radical planet whom it aspects during transit and if Saturn is the lord of Lagna or Ascendant in the natal chart, Saturn doesn't indicate any negative influence or even if it indicates any negative influence it would be just marginal and at the same time being a Lagna lord Saturn becomes a prosperity indicator.

The person should learn to keep cool and have patience. If one cannot, then he/she is succumbing to the basic nature of Saturn. One should know that Saturn alone cannot overpower the good effects of all other planets. As Dasha always takes precedence over Transit and if a good and positive Dasha/Period is ongoing the effects of the Saturn's 7½ years cycle becomes lesser. Saturn cannot act in isolation for 7½ years or eat away all good effects of the other eight planets in these 7½ years and to top it all if the deeds or Karma is good during the said period there could be in fact a good degree and extent of uplift and overall progress and prosperity during the Sade-Sati.

Saturn increases the results of the house where it resides in the horoscope and reduces the results of houses aspected by it. Saturn's negative attributes is considered for quarrel, enmity, imprisonment, murder, persisting disease, humiliation, failure, hurdles, bitterness in relationships, despair etc. Similarly Saturn's positive attributes are disciplined life, prosperity due to the individual's hard work and efforts, peaceful existence and divine protection from all kinds of troubles and issues, with Saturn's blessings no enemy can ever get successful in hurting someone and even if that happens the *Karma* hits back.

Saturn related people are suspicious, clever, churning and assertive by nature. They are serious, imaginative, entrepreneurs, frugal, persevering, lovers of freedom, inventors, reserved, lovers of astronomy and chemistry and are sensitive for honour.

Diseases like ailments of legs, accidents, impotence, wind related problems, spinal cord, cancer, bone health, and such issues are related

to Saturn. Cobblers iron smiths, mechanics, carpenters, coal traders, drivers, oil traders, judges are related to Saturn. Saturn is exalted in Tula/Libra and debilitated in Mesha/Aries. Venus and Mercury are its friends, Sun,
Moon and Mars are enemies and Jupiter is neutral.

Saturn undoubtedly connects with human sufferings intricately, but it also gives us the courage to fight adversities. No materialistic remedy can absolve an individual of Saturn's fierce impact except their own Karmic correction acts and good deeds. Materialistic remedies, like reciting Hanuman Chalisa, visiting Saturn/Shani Temple, offerings etc. might give some support but Good Karma such as social service, serving the needy, downtrodden and under-privileged etc. is the best known remedy for Sade-Sati.

Actually one gains experience from this planet, which makes him or her fit to live in the world. The position of Saturn in transit in the chart indicates the part of life that is being examined and tested at that time, in the house the Saturn is transiting represents the areas of greatest tension in one's life which requires close attention, efforts and sheer hard work. The house that Saturn transits in the natal chart represents energies in one's life that are being challenged and behaviour patterns that require examinations. When Saturn indicates some losses, separation from relations etc., these are blessings in disguise which limits one's needs which one must accept gladly.

For Saturn's transit analysis in to any particular house, whether from natal Moon sign or from natal Lagna or Ascendant, the following points must be considered.

1. The position of Saturn in birth chart, whether exalted, in Mooltrikona Rashi or Sign, Own or friendly Sign.

2. The ownership of Saturn for different Ascendants or Moon sign, whether benefic, malefic or Yogakaraka etc.

3. When a planet is strong in birth chart but weak in transit it will indicate neutral results or vice versa. It will not indicate much loss, worries etc. to the individual.

4. When Saturn is weak in birth chart and in transit is in same house malefic results can be indicated.

5. The aspects of Saturn on other planets and vice versa are to be considered, whether the aspects are malefic or benefic. The aspect of Jupiter on Saturn can change malefic results to benefic.

Good Aspects, when Saturn forms good aspects with other planets, namely trine, sextile, etc. will indicate that one would be careful, attentive, sober, calculative, exacting, could benefit from increased income and comforts, peace of mind, methodical working, acquisition of property, profitable and gainful connections.

Bad Aspects, when Saturn forms a negative aspect with planets, that indicates that the individual could get some sudden and unexpected outcomes which could be the result of his/her actions either in this this life or the previous incarnations. Such transiting Saturn could indicate period of limitation, restriction, possible ill health, depleted energy, losses, depressive moods, general misfortune. Yet can also be a useful time for wise and long-term planning, conserving energy, building up resources, study, serious contemplation of life and self. Patience is the key word here, which will be needed as this is not a time to push ahead with plans and affairs, and forcing matters will not do much good. It is better to accept that this aspect would slow down the rhythm of life with respect to the attributes and characteristics of the house or planet involved, showing which lessons of discipline and structure must be learned. A time to consolidate and prepare for more to go-ahead with the indications in the chart.

It should be kept in mind that the Astrology principles should not be applied verbatim or followed as a rule literally, but be analysed in view of the all the above mentioned points, which would save from untoward and uncalled for mental anguish and worries.

During transit, Saturn will indicate good effects in 3rd, 6th, and 11th houses. The broadly applicable and general effects of Saturn are mentioned here, which again should be modified as per aspects conjunctions and rules of transit, in a holistic manner.

Saturn's transit in 1st house or Lagna

The position and the period when Saturn transits over the Ascendant, is a time deep introspection of the aspects of life, responsibilities could increase and accomplishments could be good. It is advisable not to start any new long range projects, which could get delayed and may not get completed on time if started, short term projects should be prioritised. Procrastination should be avoided at all costs. Introspect for any lapses in discipline and order in life and try to correct them. It is the time of introspection. An excellent time for any kind of psycho-therapy or human potential work. A functionally malefic Saturn's transit of the first house means the person receives relatively lesser favours from others and may also have lack of confidence. It is a time of little luck, abundance, or fortune. As Saturn transits the first house, it aspects the third, seventh, and tenth houses. The tenth house aspect combined with the first house influence strongly indicates little chance of advancement in worldly matters. The aspect to the third house signifies restriction in fulfilling day to day desires, difficulties with communication, siblings, and low vitality. Saturn's glance on the seventh house means restricted opportunities for new love relationships and obstacles or strife in married life. During these approximately two-and-a-half years, the head is susceptible to injury or affliction. A functionally benefic Saturn would indicate positive things overall.

Health-wise, the person may feel tired, lifeless, and lacking in vitality. He/she should get plenty of rest, exercise, and fresh air, and maintain a healthy lifestyle. If they indulge in poor living habits during this period, would certainly pay a price. The person should avoid overworking and excessively stressful situations. It is a good time to take care of personal health. The person may be criticized or reprimanded about his/her appearance and should now consider exactly what image he/she wishes to project to the world. For those who are overweight, it is an easy time to thin out. Because they would feel serious and sombre during this transit, the person should include plenty of recreation and entertainment in his/her life.

This period favours all efforts at personal discipline and psychological integration. The person may succeed in transforming his/her personality, correcting bad habits, and beginning new practices and customs. Their body may demand attention, and it is an excellent time to start exercise programs, fitness regimens, necessary diets, and so on. The person would make serious advances in psychological work, counselling, or therapeutic techniques. They may feel that the growth is slow, tedious, and perhaps even imperceptible. However, the changes which could happen would be genuine, lasting, and meaningful. The power of one's consciousness directed on the self cannot help but bring about maturity and self-knowledge. By the time this transit is over, the person is older, wiser, and more objective about himself/herself. They would relinquish long-held illusions, fantasies, and deceptions about his identity and personality.

Although Saturn's transit of the first house is not quite a good time to launch new ventures, especially if the Saturn is functionally malefic in the concerned chart otherwise it is one of the finest periods for the person to learn about his/her ultimate objectives and desires. Therefore, they do well in restructuring their existence and modifying the direction of their life. However, it would be recommended that they need to be patient about results and need not expect current actions to bear too much fruit for some time to come. Throughout this transit, the person could feel pressured to come to terms with his/her identity and to do the right thing regarding their life. In other words, they would be compelled to act in accord with their individual purpose and calling. And while they may feel frightened or overwhelmed, the person would then be in the proper frame of mind to accept full responsibility for his/her destiny. Despite the unyielding tension and pressure the person feels during this transit, that he/she has an unusually objective perspective and would be generally be free to rethink, re-choose, and re-embrace the life he/she chose in this life. The task may not be painless, but the opportunity could be profound.

When Saturn transits the first house, the person would be drawn inward to work on his/her personality, character, and internal makeup. He/she tries to perfect the most essential way of being, and roots out character flaws, shortcomings, and weaknesses. This is an excellent time for introspection, contemplation, and honest self-evaluation. However, it is a tedious and difficult period for worldly matters, no matter how much energy the person expends towards outer accomplishments, he/she experiences relatively lesser support of nature. Indeed, the opposite could be the case depending on the functional nature of Saturn as per the individual chart/horoscope. There could be lesser chance that the person is likely to receive awards, promotions, or significant advancements if the Saturn is functional malefic in the chart but it could be just opposite if Saturn is functional benefic in the horoscope. He/she must proceed with caution, prudence, and discretion, because his/her actions could readily meet with resistance and opposition during this period. The person could be continually thrown back onto themselves to examine the motives and reflect upon them. He/she should not look for significant achievement other than the behavioural and psychological gains he/she makes.

Saturn's transit in 2nd house

This is the time when there could be advancement in psychological, spiritual and moral values. If Saturn is malefic there could be loss of wealth, thus care should be taken during this time. One should exert better control over your material possessions by working hard to keep everything going on as required. There could be times when fear of financial security could be there during this period. This is one of the best periods to organise one's finances and get involved stream lining and bringing in discipline in money matters.

The second house represents food, speech, education, wealth, family and matters. Thus, the person could get in to issues related to domestic matters, difficulties in school, and some issues with earnings and/or investments. He/she may also have problems with the right eye, if Saturn is functionally malefic. As Saturn transits the second house, it aspects the fourth, eighth, and eleventh houses. The fourth house glance indicates restrictions or tediousness with homes, cars, comforts, happiness, mother, and progress in education etc. and there could be pretty good progress if Saturn is functionally benefic for the concerned horoscope. The aspect to the eighth house indicates loss or sudden gains, or some profits and/or losses, and potential problems with the reproductive system. Occult studies are not much favoured at this time, however with favourable aspect of Jupiter the same can also be undertaken, it should also be remembered that in any case a favourable aspect of benefic Jupiter cancels and negates many negative indications. Saturn's aspect on the eleventh house restricts financial success from side ventures if malefic and profits if benefic. It also means the person could have differences with his friends and acquaintances, and could have a very difficult time fulfilling important long-term goals and desires.

When Saturn transits the second house, the person could concentrate on wealth, possessions, and self-worth. This period also brings a good deal of self-analysis and self-examination. The main difference between Saturn's transit in Lagna and the second house is that while self-worth and deservedness are sensitive and intimate issues, the person would be now more outwardly directed during this transit. He/she is consumed with financial pressures and requirements, focuses mainly on making money, meeting expenses, and, if he/she is lucky, collecting his/her share of material benefits. Therefore, this transit is experienced could be seen as a practical and materialistic phase. The person finds himself/herself engaged in a quest for financial security.

The person should be made aware during this transit that there is a deeper significance to his/her pursuit of wealth. Though they appear simply to be responding to circumstances, they are, in fact, being driven to confront confidence issues. The connection between their self-worth and the wealth they are able to create becomes obvious now. Income is very likely to be restricted, and the resultant financial pressure causes the person to look deeply into his/her feelings and beliefs about themselves. When they cannot meet expenses, they could question their own fitness and worth. This transit makes

the person take responsibility for creating a healthy sense of self-worth. Certain individuals could make more money than ever before during this period as a result of a true
self-confidence and diligent, effective efforts to gain wealth during several previous years.

For those who habitually ignore the concept of affluence or neglect material needs, these two-and-a-half years may be extra difficult. The person may suddenly find himself/herself struggling under the weight of debt, deficits, and old bills during this period if Saturn is functionally malefic in the horoscope. They must now squarely face the importance of money in life. Some people decide to place great attention on earning wealth, either to gain a greater feeling of security or to ensure freedom and independence in the years to come. In any event, financial responsibility is essential during this period. This is a poor time for gambling, get-rich quick schemes, or high-risk investments. The person should especially avoid extravagant spending. He/she should work on building resources and creating a solid foundation of capital. They must learn the value of receiving proper rewards for the efforts and decide exactly what part money plays in their priorities. By the end of this transit, the person could realise that before he/she can enjoy any of life's pleasures, he/she must first be able to meet the basic financial needs and feel good about themselves. For this reason, the transit is a profoundly important one.

Saturn's transit in 3rd house

This transit period is time for improving environment in and around one's daily life and inculcating a habit of positive thinking so that the constructive approach benefits life in many ways. There could be opportunities for extensive changes, even if one does not realise them. There would be good support from relations, close friends and other acquaintances during this time and the opportunities for development and progress would be there with of course hard work and effort. During this transit, one could be successful, there could be pleasant functions, recognition of service, positive events, positive reports, gain of wealth, pleasure, prosperity and success in undertakings. All round happiness, power, position and enjoyments could be the possibilities if Saturn is aspected by benefic planets.

The third house represents energy, willpower, communication, risk taking ability, patience and the ability to fulfil one's daily desires. Therefore, the person has difficulty accomplishing simple goals and minor tasks. He/she works diligently. They are, in fact, learning how to make the most efficient use of energy, as minor obstacles interfere with their intentions during this transit period. During Saturn's transit of the third house, it aspects the fifth, ninth, and twelfth houses. The aspect to the fifth could indicate tedious experiences with pregnancy, children, and investments. The aspect to the ninth indicates restricted luck and travel, difficulties with religious or spiritual teachers, and hardship in gaining any higher knowledge. Saturn's aspect on the twelfth house signifies many debts and expenses, misfortune at foreign and remote places, and strong discipline to pursue enlightenment.

When Saturn transits the third house, the person delves deeply into knowledge and tries to learn all he/she can in order to better his/her existence. This would be a time of profound focus and concentration in school or any kind of career training. The person may conduct research, analysis, or other investigative projects. His/her thinking will be deep, profound, and serious. They must, however, beware of depression and a sombre attitude.

Recreation, amusements, and hobbies can counter the person's laborious, concentrated mental activity. Saturn's transit of the third house signifies an unusual drive to reach out and connect with others. The person may encounter obligations and responsibilities with siblings and relatives. He/she will feel a powerful need to communicate with friends, peers, and loved ones. The person would be compelled to extract all manner of detailed truths and to share the findings with those who will listen. They would tend to write more letters, messages, and bulletins than ever before during this period, may explore the possibility of writing in magazines and journals. Such activities may not flow with great spontaneity, but they spring from a sense of urgency, importance, and purpose.

The person's daily habits and attitudes now demand attention. They suddenly view their experience with microscopic perception, and everything seems to slow down. The person witness his/her behaviour with more detachment than usual and observes that many of his/her actions and undertakings do not produce all that he/she wants and deserves. The quality of their life is would be about to make serious progress. They begin to examine everything outside themselves in a fresh and objective way. During this transit period the person spends these two-and-a-half years determining what information he/she needs in order to live successfully. And then he/she vigorously educates himself/herself.

The person makes excellent use of the plentiful knowledge that comes his/her way. They would be capable of structuring their ideas and opinions better than ever. Educators, intellectuals, and those who use their minds to earn a living may feel burdened by this transit, because the mind is strained. But this period brings powerful insights, and the person would improve cognitive power in a way that benefits profoundly in the years to come. Health-wise, the lungs and nervous system are vulnerable during this period. The person feels a great responsibility toward his/her environment and they would do their best to avoid worrying, although they may have to constantly deal with minor details, trivial matters, and unimportant problems.

By the time this transit is over, the person would have grasped the need for precision and learned to think along with strengthening rational thinking process and significantly increasing the ability to function objectively. As a result, they are more flexible and able to function within the often paradoxical world in which they live. They would shift their attention from knowledge to a more instinctual experience.

Saturn's transit in 4th house

An important transit as the fourth house indicates education, mother, ability to think deeply and focus, domestic life, conveyance and vehicles and many other attributes. Domestic issues could become critical which one should solve with a calm approach. This period could trigger simple reorganising to major reshuffling of one's relations and connections in domestic life. There could be some sudden development with respect one's house which could be pending payments, or some repairs and services etc. Past incidents which could not be settled may have something to do during this period and play their prominence and Saturn's transit in the fourth house is especially good time to resolve all such pending issues. Start modestly to gain and rise. Some negative factors at work or in education could oppose one's successful achievements as Saturn aspects the tenth house from this fourth house, whose one of the attributes is profession or career.

Saturn's transit of this house would be an arduous one. As it moves through the Fourth house, it aspects the sixth, tenth, and first houses. As a result, restrictions, obstacles, and delays in health resolution, daily work, career success, promotions, and any type of personal luck or favouritism could occur. It is a good period to engage in discipline, self-control, spiritual austerities, and organisational assignments. The fourth house also indicates matters related to heart which could indicate resultant heart issues. When Saturn transits through the fourth house, it aspects the first, tenth, and sixth houses. The aspects to the tenth and first powerfully inhibit gain in the world if Saturn is functionally malefic and gains if Saturn is functionally benefic for the chart/horoscope.

During this transit, the person spends time building the foundation for his/her future success and achievement. It is a time of slow, concentrated effort to ensure one's ultimate security in the material world. This is one of the least rewarding transits of all for increase, gain, promotion, and all outer signs of

Accomplishment, if Saturn is functionally malefic else opposite indications can be expected. The person is engrossed in a natural state of introversion and introspection lives life from the perspective of ancestral values, hereditary talents, and security/survival concerns. The person is focused on his/her most fundamental nature and instincts. They should now be seeking to plan, build, organize, structure, and save. If they are expecting abundance, luck, and prosperity, they are likely to be sorely disappointed with a malefic Saturn else would get duly rewarded.

Difficulties involving the person's habitat and living conditions may surface at the onset of this transit. The person directs his/her attention to the home space and residential location. They must make all necessary improvements to their home and conveyances. Situations could arise which guide the person to consider whether they live in the area best suited to their nature and needs. This would be the optimum time to learn lessons and responsibility about land, homes, and property. If the person moves during this transit period he/she may likely do so out of a sense of duty, and the move may seem burdensome. Moves during Saturn transits occur only out of definite purpose and necessity, and happen less frequently than when Jupiter transits or aspects the fourth house. Moves during Jupiter influences produce buoyancy, happiness, pleasure, and luck, while moves during Saturn's transit generate security, safety, and a solid ground for one's future base of operations.

The person's major concerns would be personal and intimate, and he would work diligently to safeguard his/her future peace and tranquillity. They would be sensitive to domestic issues and family needs and may have problems or increased responsibilities with parents, and more likely with mother. This transit may be somewhat unfavourable for mother's health if she is old and sick, if Saturn is functionally malefic. Expansion of public life or community affairs are not much favoured. The fourth house also relates to family life and genetic inheritances, and so on. Therefore, this would be a good time to engage in psychological healing techniques.

More than ever before, the person has access to memories of his/her upbringing and early childhood. They begin to realize how individuality, personality, and psyche has been shaped by their background, parents, and friends circle. As this awakening occurs, the person reflects, clarifies, and begins to take responsibility for all his/her inherited, unconscious behaviour. He/she would take stock of his/her origins, confronts internal connections and makes some of the greatest personal and psychological advances of his/her life. Planets transiting through the fourth house bring a person in touch with his/her innate, instinctive being. Transformations made during this period occur on a subtle level, and produce lasting, tangible effects.

Saturn's transit in 5th house

This period of Saturn's transit in the fifth house is a time for the individual to proceed in a careful and organised manner in whatever he/she does and they need to communicate freely and in a tactful way such that they should not reveal everything without being asked. During this period there could be some minor issues with respect to children either education or their health etc. and if functionally Saturn is benefic and has no Vedha in this transit the children could excel in their field and would bring happiness and satisfaction. If the individual has love affairs, they may go through some difficult times such as some mis-understandings etc. which calls for careful approach in such delicate matters and if dealt wisely, it could be advantageous. During this transit heavy investments are not advised if Saturn is functionally malefic and there could be some losses in trading, if involved. Any risky ventures are best avoided during this time. Hard work and living an organised and disciplined life should be adhered to as far as possible during this period.

When Saturn transits the fifth house, it aspects the seventh, eleventh, and second houses. The aspects to the seventh and eleventh houses could limit the person's ability to fulfil his/her ambitions and cravings. He/she may have difficulties with groups and friends, and may encounter restrictions or problems with his/her spouse. If the person is single, could have fewer opportunities for creating a beneficial love relationship at this time. Saturn's aspect on the second house means financial delays and obstacles, which could in turn be increased due to the weakened eleventh house of gains and profits. The fifth house indicates working of mind, stomach, digestive system and intellect Thus there could be effect on these and other related functions like depression, seriousness, or pessimism. The body could be vulnerable to digestive issues during this period. Married life and one's emotional needs may certainly be thwarted or get disturbed, due to Saturn's aspect on the seventh house. The fifth house is also known as 'Poorvapunya' or past-life credit, thus this is an important time for remembering one's destiny and considering the possibility of leadership or politics.

When Saturn transits the fifth house, the individual explores the uniqueness of the spirit. Their energy and intensity is now focused on personal creativity and self-expression. The purpose of their existence becomes their biggest concern. During this remarkably important transit, the person discovers his/her most essential talents and abilities, those which differentiate them from others. It is a good time for gaining self-knowledge and self-understanding through introspection, self-analysis, and all methods of enlightenment. The person may exercise authority as well as express themselves artistically. Individuals involved in the arts, sciences, and literary professions may experience profound results during this time as they could come into contact with their deepest creative resources during this transit. Such persons should consciously strive to make the most of this period.

There could be good and decent progress during this period, Saturn's transit of the fifth house is neither easy, pleasurable, nor fun, which depends to a great extent on the functional nature of Saturn as per the chart/horoscope of the concerned individual under evaluation. The person would feel serious, and burdened by the weight of responsibility, which if taken up sportingly would ensure a good future ahead. Development of potential and mastery of one's inherent talents should be taken up during this period. The person would be generally serious and worked up during this transit and may need to be reminded to live life normally in all its hues.

Saturn's transit brings up issues and questions of 'deserving something'. The person may undergo what feels like fate with his/her partner. The person could feel vulnerable in the realm of love and is driven to dive deep in to the meaning of these affairs and incidents. For those who find themselves suffering and undergoing tough times due to their partner, it is an especially important period. Unlike one's ordinary experience of repaying past-life debts, the person may now has the perfect psychological temperament to gain strikingly accurate insights and conclusions about what they deserve and what they do not. The individual would be objective in perceiving the ramifications of his/her past actions and behaviour.

Many individuals during this transit could feel that they are not loved and appreciated, and may also lack in energy, enthusiasm, and confidence. In such cases, the individual must confront the reasons of the matter and make whatever changes are necessary. Such effects are, of course, could be due to the person's subtle and innermost feelings. This is one of the best transits of all, for transforming one's pride, dignity, self-respect, and self-worth. It is also a time to consider one's potential and likelihood for fame and leadership. The person evaluates his/her standing in the world and may feel a strong sense of determination and willpower, and feel compelled to follow their own instincts, desires, and heart at this time. During this transit all forms of gambling and speculation should be avoided, as Saturn's passage through the fifth house dampens one's buoyancy and luck in such matters.

There may be also restriction, burden, difficulties, and grief because of children and youngsters during this transit. Health-wise, the heart could be vulnerable or under pressure.

Saturn's transit in 6th house

This transit is a good and positive period for the individual and during this period he/she would generally win over their opponents in every field and level. There would be general gains, success in education, service or business. Good health would prevail and all round prosperity would be there. There would chances to gain wealth and if married, would lead a happy married life. This transit is a critical time in one's development, as they could receive some recognition of the work done, which could further mean a time of heavy responsibility and hard work. If in service one must rise to the demands and expectations of the management which if achieved could result in recognition, gains and rewards.

Saturn transit in the sixth house, it aspects the eighth, twelfth, and third houses. The aspects to the eighth and twelfth houses could indicate some troubles and disturbances with sexual enjoyment, debts and expenses, and wills and legacies. This is generally not a good time to borrow or spend money. Saturn's aspect on the third house, could indicate difficulties and frustration with siblings, risk potential and communication as well as limited energy to fulfil one's daily desires and ambitions.

When Saturn transits the sixth house, the person learns the value of daily work. He/she also becomes accountable for his/her health, appearance and habits. Circumstances may arise which require the person to work harder, longer, and more diligently than any other time in the past. They would improve their habitual methods and procedures and would find better ways to accomplish their goals and they would be more organized than ever.

He/she may experience difficulties and frustration at the hands of co-workers, employers, or both. The person may have to work harder than those around him/her. Yet, he/she may receive conspicuously little acknowledgement or appreciation. Misdeeds or shoddy work could be immediately noticed, and the person may not be able to avoid censure. At times he/she may even be unjustly reprimanded. Their task during this transit period could be to become conscious, perceptive, and wise in the workplace, a realm characteristically comprised of habit, routine, and dedicated focus.

The individual may find himself/herself working at a job which is tedious and restrictive, a job incapable of generating fulfilment and satisfaction. In some cases, the person may decide to quit, choosing unemployment over monotonous, unstimulating work. However, such a response is only wise if the person is seriously seeking a better situation. If he/she is merely trying to avoid pressure and struggle in the workplace, he/she may lose valuable lessons and experiences and be less successful in the years to come.

During this transit, the person may become discriminating. He/she may begin to examine all of his/her habits and private rituals. They may rapidly develop a strong sense of patience which allows them to plan and design their life more efficiently. Practical matters such as health, diet, and clothing become especially important during this transit period. For individuals who do not wish to focus on details and mundane concerns, life may feel tedious and tiresome. However, this would be the perfect time to take responsibility for health and all personal concerns. This is Saturn's last passage through a house charactering personal attributes and the person need to strengthen and fortify himself/herself.

Fitness regimens and exercise programs would take a priority place in life during this transit time as sixth house mainly indicates health aspects of the individual. Any weak or vulnerable bodily functions may immediately break down at the onset of this transit in order to be finally corrected. The person should address chronic illnesses in a serious and committed manner. Although health matters for some may be difficult and demanding during this transit period, by the end of this transit the person may have completely transformed his/her relationship to their physical well-being.
In short, the person becomes aware of his/her responsibility for taking care of his/her body. This is a good time for organisation, skill, efficiency, service oriented concerns, and the study of medicine or any other healing methods. However, the person may have troubles with servants, maids, house-helps, and subordinates.

Saturn's transit in 7th house

The partner, relations and close associates could have too many demands during this period, which will be difficult for the individual to handle. There is a likelihood of some relationships going sour on this account. In some cases temporarily married life could affected, if the seventh lord is badly placed and has malefic connections and influence. Co-workers, colleagues and in some cases friends would be demanding too much than in the past.

Every attempt should be made to keep up the agreements and contracts made with others or else there could be likelihood to a good extent of negative ramifications, basically discipline, order and adherence needs to be maintained. There could be some disturbances in travel plans and things may not go as expected, which calls for thinking about all possible contingencies while planning the journeys.

When Saturn transits the seventh house, it aspects the ninth, first, and the fourth houses. The first house aspect means the person could get a feeling of restrictions in various spheres of life. They would be unlikely be favoured, get any recognitions etc., win awards, or enjoy promotions, if Saturn is functionally malefic. It is very important to check whether Saturn is functionally malefic or benefic to get an indication of the expected results. Generally Saturn is attributed and given all negative indications, but it is not so, Saturn does indicate tremendous positivity in some cases. The aspects to the ninth and fourth houses signifies difficulties or limited fulfilment with travel, religious or spiritual teachers, land, homes, and parents. The indications could be positive and uplifting as well if Saturn is functionally benefic.

This transit often indicates karmic relationships which feel predestined and which are highly significant to the person's overall growth process. The person's ability to love could get tested to the limit. He/she may be attracted to older, authoritarian lovers. By the end of this transit, the person could understand love as something much greater than mere emotions, sensations, or a happy state of mind. This is a good time to deal squarely with issues of Personal characteristics and love matters.

Single individuals who are seek committed relationship may find themselves in one of the intense love relationships of their lives. Some would realize that it is time to lower unrealistic standards or relinquish certain requirements and finally materialise their goal. Therefore, marriage is a distinct possibility. Some, in this situation, however, could get foiled by deep-rooted problems which require counselling or therapy. In these cases, the person may attract a partner by whom he/she could be profoundly captivated. They might feel certain that they have found the perfect soul mate, the one they would be destined to marry, which could be an apparent matter and exists only in order to reveal the person's inadequacies in the realm of love. Because of the person's extreme desire to have his/her special partner, the person may finally may obtain some outside help which has been long needed.

When Saturn, the planet of karma and justice, transits the seventh house, the person is forced to confront whatever lessons are needed in the area of love, relationship and partnership. Some individuals experience a time of few or no love or relationship opportunities at all, and feel profound loneliness. Though such effects could be the consequence of negative actions from past lifetimes or previous deeds, this may not be always the case. Most often, the person could be being blatantly pressured to take responsibility for creating love or relationship by socializing, or else to suffer the consequences of their self-induced isolation. During this transit, also some individuals may find that they are well suited to a single life. And those who are involved in extramarital affairs or improper situations may get revealed during this transit.

When Saturn transits the seventh house, the individual learns to take responsibility for his/her love life. Their marriage, or primary love relationship, will be the most important area for growth during the period of this transit. During this period, the person could define the most essential and specific need of the heart. They learn the true meaning of flexibility and also learn to compromise with their cherished one. The person could also get in to some frictions with the loved ones or could be called to task for inappropriate or unloving conduct especially if the Saturn is a functional malefic in the concerned horoscope. All of the limitations, restrictions, and imperfections in the area of the heart are laid bare by circumstances and the partner, so that the person may now improve his/her behaviour. During this period, the person could be unusually objective about his/her shortcomings in such matters, and is more than willing to mend his/her ways. They feel a deep and profound sense of responsibility toward the partner during this period.

Saturn's transit of the seventh house is an certain time for commitment or recommitment to one's spouse or partner. If the person is involved in an easy-going, non-committed relationship, he/she now may have to determine during this period whether to deepen their involvement or to eliminate it altogether. They perceive the domestic life clearly and practically during this time. If his/her situation is a hopeless one, with no harmonious future in sight, the individual could become quickly aware that he/she must end his/her predicament. Saturn drives the individual to do the right thing with respect to relationship during this period and to take necessary action.

Saturn's transit in 8th house

During this period there could be some issues with finances and possessions one has with others. There could be some disagreement with others and there may be a chance that the resources of others being utilised by the individual may be cut off, thus during this transit of Saturn the individual should carefully think and plan his/her finances and resources such that during an event of critical requirement things are available. The person should plan for self-dependence during this period as far as possible. Chronic health issues should b taken care of during this period as they may take vigorous form with a little carelessness. This period generally teaches an individual how to deal with people and also exposes some inner and true characteristics of people we deal with. There could be some chance of a separation from family or near and dear ones.

When Saturn transits the eighth house, it aspects the tenth, second, and fifth houses. Thus there may be difficulties, delays, and obstacles in the realms connected to these houses if Saturn is a functional malefic and improvement and progress if Saturn is a functional benefic for the chart. The person could have a hard time expanding his/her career and increasing the wealth. Investments may not get favoured, nor are dealings with children. This would be a time of responsibility, discipline, and preparation for one's duty in worldly matters.

During this transit, the person has more patience, persistence, and perseverance for research and investigation. He/she becomes more aware of other people's values, principles, and standards, and learns how to peacefully coexist with them. By the end of this transit, the person would have eliminated certain ineffective or life-damaging habit patterns.

Saturn's transit through the eighth house is generally a not so conducive time for money from partners or gains from wills, legacies, insurance companies, and lending institutions. If at all possible, the person should be alerted before this transit to organize his financial affairs and to eliminate all past debts, monetary obligations, and undesired economic partnerships. Affairs stemming from joint finances and previous borrowing may bring feelings of burden and stress at this time. It is a poor time to borrow money or undertake new financial risks or ventures. Instead, the person should attend to his/her financial responsibility within existing deals and partnerships. The person should update his/her will, clarify the economic situation, and inform his/her loved ones of all necessary information, facts and figures which they might need in case of his/her death.

During this period the person acutely feels his/her mortality and ponders the fact that human life is temporary and can end at any moment. The issues of death and the after-life suddenly become important. Though this transit may coincide with the death of friends or relatives, such occurrences are not a foregone conclusion. However, if death occurs within the person's circle, he/she would be more probable to attend the funeral and may comply as well. As a result, the person gains knowledge, wisdom, and a degree of preparation for death and dying. This transit is the time to earnestly reflect on the mysteries of life and matters of the soul. The person gains significant spiritual growth and may directly experience metaphysical or occult incidents.

During Saturn's transit of the eighth house, the individual could learn lessons about sex and procreation and may experience temporary sexual issues and difficulties in his/her sex life. Because of these effects, they could decide to pay conscious attention to physical passions and their impact. During this time the individual could feel a sense of discipline and duty in a previously instinctive, organic realm. They may wish to investigate the field of sexuality, as well as examine their own bodily abilities and carnal

techniques. The person would be more aware than ever of the power of sex during this time. He/she would be conscious of the effects of their sexual activities on themselves and others.
During this period, they may be celibate, or at could be quite deliberate in the use of their sexuality. The individual realises during this time, the potential energy drain of sexual carelessness or misconduct. If they are involved in a physically unsatisfying relationship or marriage, sexual matters could worsen at the onset of the transit until they address the issue and make necessary adjustments.

When Saturn transits the eighth house, the person purifies his/her desire nature and his/her use of power. They could be pressured from outside forces to contemplate the motives as well as their methods of achieving goals and attaining fulfilment. Manipulative or domineering habit patterns could get exposed and attacked by others, and they must now root out such tendencies. In general Saturn is all about ethical and honest behaviour, these two aspects protect the individual even when Saturn is functionally malefic. This period is potentially a time of great emotional vulnerability. The person could be extra sensitive to criticism and may feel compelled to correct any compulsive or obsessive features of his/her character that could be founded upon deep attachments and unconscious desires. This transit duration may bring significant psychological pain, depending upon how willing the person is to deal with trust and control issues, if Saturn is functionally malefic else the situation would be normal. They may feel their individuality being curbed or pressured out of existence. By the end of this transit, much of his/her personality could get transformed, and the person would be healthier, more psychologically balanced, and emotionally free. Having purified his/her desires, the person is less bound by unconscious motives and behaviours.

Saturn's transit in 9th house

During Saturn's transit in the ninth house there could be some problems or difficulties on the legal side particularly if there is a malefic Vedha on 9th house and if there is a malefic connection to the ninth house in the natal chart. There could be some possibility of unexpected long travels which could be beneficial if there is a benefic influence on the ninth house and if there is no Vedha and the travels could be troublesome and may incur some losses if there is Vedha and also if there is some malefic connection to the ninth house in the natal chart. Religious activities could take the focus during this period making the individual to ponder over spirituality and philosophy. Learning would be quite pragmatic during this time. Opponents may not be able to create troubles during this time. May indicate some health issues to father during this time.

When Saturn transits the ninth house, it aspects the eleventh, third, and sixth houses, thus the person could experience some issues in the realms ruled by these houses, if Saturn is functionally malefic or else the ride would be smoother. Due to the aspect on the third and eleventh, there could be delays, obstacles, and complications with friends and siblings, if Saturn is functionally malefic. Since the third and eleventh are the desire houses, the person may experience some temporary difficulties and setbacks in fulfilling goals and ambitions. Saturn's aspect on the sixth house indicates stress in the workplace and pressure on the person's health.

The person would seek an intense and concentrated learning experience. He/she may return to school or any serious training program during this period of transit. They would like to master whatever practice or profession they would be working on previously. They would discover the most realistic and practical methods for their work, beliefs, and philosophies. This would be another opportunity to perfect abilities and expertise and to put them into fruitful action. The individual would get ready for Saturn's

Next transit to his/her professional domain that is the tenth house when he/she can gain the greatest professional authority, reputation, and prestige.

During this transit period, the person will have aspirations to expand his/her awareness, knowledge, and experience. More than this, he/she may feel a desire to spread his/her influence far and wide. They may travel to foreign countries for business or professional interests. The person will feel pressured to disseminate any knowledge, information, or writings which they would have been delaying to perform or do. Commitment comes to the fore, even if by pressure which would ensure good progress in future.

The person could travel long distances for serious, philosophical, or educational purposes. The person is now committed to finding truth. His/her faith could get tested. They may undergo ordeals, trials, and tribulations that test their values and morals. The person will delve deeply into all the wisdom he/she would have gained throughout life. During this period the individual would tend to practice spirituality in general in their day to day lives. Their ability to translate faith into action could get challenged and they would spend time to examine their concepts of right and wrong. They may face difficulties, delays, or obstacles in foreign countries or remote places in order to broaden their perspective and to learn the underlying reasons for customs and practices of other cultures.

When Saturn transits the ninth house, the person searches for the meaning of life. He/she tries to understand the significance of existence and discover where he/she fits into the larger scheme of things. The person would spend most of the time during this transit defining his/her beliefs, value and morals. They may get engaged in serious discussion about various things including religion, philosophy, and all kinds of higher knowledge. During this transit the person would be especially discriminating in his/her choice of gurus, mentors and teachers. They may or may not accept the views and opinions of others easily and may also challenge people frequently. There may be significant disappointment, disillusionment, or frustration in the person's understandings especially if Saturn is a functional malefic.

Saturn's transit in 10th house

This is an important transit to a sensitive point that is the zenith of one's natal chart, which covers the professional life, material acquisitions etc. during this transit the individual would gain many responsibilities.
If an individual is a leader, a politician, a businessman, a trader etc. He/she would achieve

success and the responsibilities if taken up and carried on, they would be mostly successful and if they shirk the responsibility could see negative results during this transit. A fit time to make one's impression upon others. Negative energies could cause disaster and it is possible to fall through one's own actions. In case there are malefic aspects to the tenth house in the natal chart, the results and indications could get modified a bit but mostly the individual would sail through this transit. The person can control the indications of this transit by preparing carefully and not taking any short cuts. His/her prestige, status, job can be maintained in a stable manner only by adhering to one's duties diligently and with greater responsibility. They would be able to handle disputes and adverse atmosphere and any untoward incidents with some preparation and should be careful against these during this transit, which indicates both positive and negative attributes.

During the transit of Saturn in the tenth house, it the twelfth, fourth, and seventh houses. The twelfth house aspect means more debts and expenses than usual and the possibility of loss from thieves and robbers, if Saturn is functionally malefic. The person would be more in to spiritualism. He/she may have difficulties in remote places or foreign countries. Saturn's fourth house glance indicates problems or restrictions associated with the person's mother or family, again the maleficence of Saturn should be checked in the concerned horoscope for every characteristic and indication and if Saturn is benefic functionally in the concerned chart, above mentioned negative indications would not be there instead there would be positive indications and progress in the related areas of the houses. Similarly the Saturn's aspect to the seventh house signifies less happiness in married life, or, for single individuals, little opportunity for marriage or a satisfying relationship.

If the person is a responsible and effective in his/her profession and career, then he/she could be recognized and acknowledged by superiors during this transit or else he/she may have difficulties with them or suffer misfortune on their behalf. In some cases, where the person would have gained prominence and success illegally or immorally, this transit may bring public disgrace or downfall as Saturn is all about justice, truth, honesty, law and order. At the beginning of this transit, the person may experience some discord, restriction, or limitation from some of either of his/her parents and one of them may begin to behave strictly or severely or they may withdraw emotional support. Such behaviour may not come to fruition, if the transit occurs during early childhood.

This transit is a time of powerful personal integration as the person is so much more detached and objective about the significance of rank, honour, and status, as they can properly determine what they are willing to do to achieve them and what he is not. The individual discovers their real commitment in life, by observing society's response to their performance. The person works diligently and unrelentingly and remarkably as he/she is not emotionally affected by success or failure during this transit. Therefore, the person can do his/her best, most efficient work-ever. Furthermore, they would be exceptionally disciplined, organized, and purposeful during this period.

This period almost always brings frustration as well and unfortunately, no individual responds flawlessly to every obstacle along the way. The person finds out exactly where he/she has miscalculated or failed, and why. The good news would be that he/she would be crystal clear about who he/she as they would understand their position and place in the society and what they must do in the future to fulfil the goals. The bad news could be that any unrealized professional ambitions could bring special disappointment. Again the beneficence or maleficence of Saturn should be checked functionally from the concerned chart/horoscope.

If the person has worked diligently toward career goals for some time, he/she would now stand a good chance of making a big impact. They may receive a leadership or organizational position because their superiors would suddenly recognize and appreciate their wisdom and experience. Certain individuals could reach the peak of their professional life at this time. But this could be more probable during Saturn's second or third transit of the tenth house and it is important for the person to have organized his/her personal life well before this transit, because their career responsibilities could seriously increase during this time. They may be downright compulsive in working on career goals and taking advantage of their newfound worldly influence and hence they need be careful not to offend family, friends, and loved ones by their neglect. The person's workload would be high and his/her time most precious.

When Saturn transits the tenth house, the person could take responsibility for his/her life calling and becomes accountable for previous career and/or professional efforts. He could either get rewards, promotions, and credit for the good he/she has done or criticism, demotions, and condemnation for ineffective or damaging professional actions and little response at all for inertia and inaction. This is an important transit because the person becomes would be sensitive to his/her status and position while receiving feedback from the world. He/she would be committed to determining their position within society and precise role in their chosen vocation. During this transit of two and a half years, the person would be able to see his/her career performance more realistically than ever. If he/she has been living under any delusions or misconceptions about their efficiency, they now come face to face with the truth of the matter. It is important to note that the person does not necessarily reap either excessive praise or rejection. In many cases, very little happens externally. But what does happen is of utmost importance to the person. Because he/she would be so committed to his/her calling, he/she analyses all feedback fully. He/she contemplates whether his/her achievements and accomplishments are valid and whether he/she truly deserves what he/she has reaped. They want to achieve their true status and fulfil their personal destiny.

Saturn's transit in 11th house

Saturn's transit in the eleventh house from natal Moon indicates a positive, gainful and uplifting time in the life of the individual. There could be gain of money, fulfilment of desires, acquisition of property, settlement of marriage and domestic happiness could be some of the attributes during this time of the transit. Also gain of fame, promotion, honour, awards and enjoyment with opposite sex could also be there. Good relations could get developed from those in power. This transit generally indicates a high period in one's life. Eleventh house is a house of cooperation from colleagues and friends, hopes and wishes, ideals and objectives and for them. The relatives, friends etc. could cooperate generally in most matters as and when required. There could be opportunity for some wealth accumulation as well during this transit provided there is control over the individual's spending and pleasures etc.

Saturn's passage through the eleventh house indicates difficulties with friends, groups, and one's sibling(s) or colleagues, if the Saturn is a functional malefic. Side ventures bring little profit, and one's major goals and desires could get delayed and obstructed and the opposite if the Saturn is a functional benefic that is good relations with all or relations improve during this period. As Saturn transits the eleventh, it aspects the first, fifth, and eighth houses. The aspect to the first house indicates lack of promotion, advancement, or favouritism, as well as potential minor health problems or attacks or personality issues if Saturn is functional malefic and improvement in these areas if Saturn is a functional benefic. The fifth house glance indicates a poor time with respect to children, health and higher studies an inability to get pregnant, if Saturn is functional malefic. Saturn's eighth house aspect indicates obstacles involving joint finances, is a less favourable time for studies related to spiritualism, philosophy etc., and may indicate vulnerability of the reproductive system.

Every negative indication should get associated only if Saturn is functional malefic and if Saturn is a functional benefic indications would be positive and beneficial with respect to the attributes of the house concerned.

As the person gains clear vision of his/her most intimate and important life goals, he/she would focus on his/her relationships with others. This would be a good time to do so because friends and groups exist largely as a support system for one's values, interests, and desires. The person may also begin to think of how to best create an ideal society. They may donate time and resources to community interests or become involved in public issues and concerned with humanitarian issues and may be more altruistic than ever. Throughout Saturn's transit of the eleventh house, the person could be having an idealistic and visionary mind. He/she would be more mental in his/her approach as his/her greatest responsibility and obligations could lie in planning the future.

The person would take stock of his/her friends and the groups he/she associates with.

Problems, irritations, frustrations, and annoyances in these areas may intensify, and the person may be compelled to deal squarely with them, if Saturn is functional malefic. They would cut off detrimental friendships or those which are more work than they are worth. Solid, rewarding friendships become stronger as the person sees the value of comrades whose commitment and loyalty are great. They may also make friends with older, authoritarian, or ascetic individuals. At the same time, the person would define and set limits on the some activities which are most suitable. They would decide which groups to become more involved with and which ones to eliminate during this transit. In certain cases the person may take on group leadership or assemble his/her own domain.

During this transit the person may pause to consider a crucial consideration that what do they want out of their existence and then perceive life through various opportunities rather than those of obligation. The person may begin to design their life according to their ultimate ambitions and long term objectives. They would determine how to break away from anything that does not support their vision.

During this transit of the eleventh house, the person takes responsibility for his/her ultimate life vision. Their focus shifts from such practical matters as career, financial success, and the impact on the world to the more essential concern of what will really bring them fulfilment. This transit would be the time to draw conclusions regarding happiness, contentment and fulfilment. The person may realise that his/her bliss does not necessarily come from the achievement of logical or rational desires. Having worked on so many different realms of life in previous years, their perspective regarding all facets of life would be greater than ever. They observe that, beyond the workings of their intellect and reasoning power, they would have an indirect hint about what they really want from life. Priorities for a meaningful existence become remarkably clear.

Saturn's transit in 12th house

This transit of Saturn in the twelfth house from the natal Moon has mixed bag of indications. Some important situations and circumstances of one's life may begin to come through whether in a positive or in a negative sense, thus this period is a time when the individual should be mentally be prepared for any eventuality. Any project not being completed could get finished by the compelling circumstances. There could be relatively lesser cooperation from friends, relations and others, despite handling them in the best possible way and some may tend to withdraw from the individual, such people and instances need to be observed and recognized. The individual's efforts may not bear expected outcomes at all times. Generally one should be careful against opposing surroundings, dangers, accidents, mental agony and worries. With a little oversight heavy expenditures may have to be borne. There could be some inconveniences and disturbances during journeys during this time.

Saturn's transit of the twelfth house indicates difficulties with the left eye and large, unexpected debts and expenses, or both if Saturn is functionally malefic and if Saturn is functionally benefic it indicates sexual pleasures, harmonious personal and family life, reduction of debts, benefits from foreign trade or jobs etc. It also indicates problems or frustrations in activities involving remote foreign countries, sexual dysfunction or lack of sexual pleasure, with a functionally malefic Saturn. As Saturn transits the twelfth, it aspects the second, sixth, and ninth houses. The aspects to the second and sixth indicates restriction in the practical matters of wealth and daily work. There could be hardships involving health, education, juniors in work or seniors or other co-workers. Saturn's ninth house aspect reveals difficulty gaining higher knowledge, problems with mentors or teachers, and restricted luck in general if Saturn is functionally malefic and all positive indications in these areas if Saturn is functionally benefic.

Individuals involved in analysing their occult studies and factors would have good time. Mystical, spiritual, and occult studies are favoured at this time, and much progress can be made in these areas. Certain people may find themselves wishing to do healing work or service-oriented endeavours.

The twelfth house also represents secrets, all that is confidential and the subconscious mind. Saturn transit is a good time for clearing up psychological problems and all kinds of relationship and emotional obsessions, complexes, or phobias dating from anytime. Though the individual may be comfortable with their own peculiar thoughts and style of thinking, they would realises that it is time to put their thoughts in order. Some individuals could seek out guidance and direction while others may go to ashrams, monasteries, or convents. Inner healing is well facilitated as the person's boundaries expand to find new definitions. Old, worn-out thinking processes and styles could change and new ones may arise, although the rebuilding process may feel quite slow.

This transit of Saturn indicates that it is its cycle of the twelve houses, thus the person could find that reviewing his/her past years and attempting to complete all unfinished projects and undertakings could give him/her a better life.

This could be a time of some major decisions towards changing one's life-style. There is would be little support from nature for new undertakings. Further, the person would feel a powerful natural tendency to go within, to mentally retreat from the world. His/her attention would be focused on the inner self.

Enlightenment, or evolution of consciousness, is an experience whereby one's boundaries expand in order to appreciate the universality and oneness of all things. And while the result is blissful, the process is often unfamiliar and uncomfortable. Faith is one's only ally. As the person reaps the spiritual consequences of his/her life experience, he/she needs to have faith in the universe and enjoy whatever expansion of consciousness occurs.

When Saturn transits the twelfth house, it is time to experience life from a spiritual perspective and to integrate the growth of consciousness resulting from all the previous transits. Now that Saturn has passed through the other houses of the horoscope, the person must take stock of his/her accomplishments, achievements, and failures and contemplate the meaning of their experiences, and seek to discover their place in society and universe at large. This transit is decidedly unlike any other, and unless the person is quite mystically, spiritually, and emotionally healthy to begin with, they could be liable to feel confused or puzzled during this transit period. The person could be engaged in a process of assimilation of that he/she is supposed to be doing and no amount of rational or logical analysis could ease or accelerate the procedure. The person simply must call on his/her deepest spiritual and intuitive resources and surrender their attachments, ego, and petty individual preferences to the higher part of their nature.

Chapter 9

Transit of Sun

The Suns transits through the houses of the horoscope are relatively shorter. On average, the Sun transits a house for a month and this transit period indicates that Sun acts to spotlight and illuminate the affairs of a house.

Sun Transits the First House

The Sun illuminates one's first house or Lagna or Ascendant, for a month bringing issues surrounding one's personal identity, appearance, outward behaviour, and self-expression to the forefront. This period marks the height of one's physical solar cycle, and the individual would be in a position to make an impression on others, and to assert his/her personal influence beyond the normal boundaries. Spontaneity of expression is what this transit is about, the individual would be ready to put his/her past behind and to start afresh, where they would feel increased energy and renewed feeling of confidence, which they should take advantage of. This would be a good time to start something new and pioneering, where personal endeavours could fetch positive outcomes. This is a time to grab opportunities from every possible angle. Problems and obstacles in one's life may be overcome by bravery, self-assertion and direct approach. During this transit care should be taken in team efforts and leadership roles would take a front seat.

Sun Transits the Second House

The Sun's transit of the second house indicates effect on all or some of the attributes pertaining to the second house. For all transits of all the houses the functional nature of Sun that is, malefic or benefic as per the chart's ascendant and placement of the Sun in the natal chart should be remembered and applied for the analysis. This transit period is a time to explore and search for making new relationships, being careful in what type of food is consumed as that could have a potential on the health. This period could also be utilised for making ne connections, and paying attention to one's immediate environment. Social Interaction is emphasized during this period, and could be for the most part light-hearted. Give other people a little extra time and attention, notice their efforts on one's behalf for reciprocation, and strengthen one's connections. The individual would be curious and more alert than usual, and could be quite busy with regular errands, which could be more than usual, paperwork, calls, meetings, discussions and socialising. Some energy could be spent in understanding and adopting to the immediate environment. Siblings, neighbours, close relatives, friends and co-workers may play a more important role than usual in the person's life during this transit. One would be more interested in exploring his/her own neighbourhood. This would not be a time of adventure-seeking, rather, it would be a time of small and routine tasks close to home. This would be a time when multiple activities in multiple areas and sectors. This is the time of year when personal finances and possessions receive maximum attention. The individual would be especially resourceful during this period and he/she could find themselves enjoying attention for intellectual know-how. The ability to express and communicate their ideas would be quite important to the person during this transit period.

Sun Transits the Third House

During this transit of the Sun through the third house relations with kin and siblings could take a hit that is there would be likelihood of some kind of friction, especially if the Sun is functionally malefic else things would be more or less normal. The individual would tend to take additional risk in to his/her tasks or professional life which need to be weighed for any adverse effects and such actions could prove beneficial if the Sun is functional benefic. There would be likelihood of travels either shorter ones or longer ones and also the travels could be beneficial if the Sun is functional benefic else there could be some losses or learnings. He/she would be eager to investigate new things, whether scientific or technical. During this period the individual may try to save money and spend too much on his/her extravagance or desires, control over expenses would be better.

Sun Transits the Fourth House

During this transit period the individual needs to be careful at his/her workplace as image and status could get effected if any slip up in work takes place. One must avoid arguments with seniors and co-workers during this time. Work pressure would be high and stressful and this could have the potential to affect the work adversely. Monetarily it would be a period of fluctuating finances and one should make sure his/her savings are good. If possible one should avoid real estate dealings during this time. Domestic comforts would be at a premium during this period. Married life during this month could lack mutual understanding and rapport and some mutual compromises would be advised and in general social life will be sluggish. There could be some health issues during this period related to digestive system, head and heart and it is recommended to be careful in this regard. Short travels would be bring in benefits.

Sun Transits the Fifth House

This would be a creative and intuitive period for the individual during which he/she would be inherently and emotionally be inspired. The individual could attempt some risky ventures during this time and a carefully calculated steps are advised. There would be pleasure and amusement trips. The person would like to show off his/her skills, expertise and the best side to the public and would seek and expect appreciation. The person would generally have a good health during this time and would be ready to help others if approached. The person would get restless and will try to perform those actions which he/she would have never performed, which should be carefully undertaken else there could be unwarranted outcomes.

Sun Transits the Sixth House

During this transit the work will bear pretty good results, and the individual would overcome obstacles easily and would also be able to dominate his/her opponents, competitors etc. The person would be able to complete unfinished projects and may also initiate new projects and would gain the appreciation from his/her superiors. Financially a good time of transit and will have good potential to gain through investments and speculation. If the Sun is functionally benefic it would generally indicate good and positive results. Relations with spouse and family will be happy and enjoyable. Peace and harmony will prevail at home. The person will enjoy good comforts and social relations. This is a very good month for networking and improving one's social contacts. With success and happiness all round, one's mental and physical health will be good and free from stress and anxiety, one will enjoy life during this transit period.

Sun Transits the Seventh House

During this time of transit, the individual would have a greater need than usual to be with a partner. Bouncing ideas off someone helps the person to better understand themselves. The partner could provide a mirror for their self-discovery. During this time, it would be prudent to realize their own potential through a significant and important other person. During this transit, one should focus on balance their personal interests and objectives with their social life, or with those of a partner. The emphasis should be on "us" rather than "me". The person would need the energies, companionship, and support of other people, and they may also seek out the reciprocative support and companionship. It's Important to include others rather than to go solo for this during this time. However, bending too much to the will of another is also not advised either.

Social Interactions of a personal kind are emphasised. Circumstances could be such that his/her diplomacy skills could be required. His/her popularity would increase and reinforced by his/her ability to cooperate and harmonise. Their ego and pride would be tied up in how they relate to others. This may be one of the busy time for people who consult or work with clients.

Sun Transits the Eighth House

During the transit of Sun in the eighth house the focus is on transformation, change, sexuality, personal growth, regeneration, sudden gains or losses, resources, addictions, taxes etc. During this period the focus should be on keeping everything in right perspective and remaining connected with ground reality as this is an excellent time to create a budget or financial plan, or to rid oneself of bad habits that undermine the sense of personal power and self-mastery. Intimate and personal relationships and matters could blossom during this time and also the chances of getting in to relationships with the opposite sex become higher, which calls for being careful in that matter. The self-mastery and psychological predisposition plays a vital role during this transit. Clearing out negative thoughts or bent of mind or getting rid of any bad habits should be attempted during this period which would help in the individual in the long run. This transit could be beneficial for sudden gains if Sun is functionally benefic for the chart.

Sun Transits the Ninth House

During this transit, more than any other time during the year, the individual would feel most adventurous and willing to take a leap of faith. This transit time and is a cycle in which one seeks higher meaning to his/her life, and/or seek out new experiences that take him/her beyond the material level and beyond the mundane details of day-to-day life. Anything that broadens the experiences gets attracted during this time. A lack of superficiality finds the individual straight to the point interested in the truth of things. It would be wise for them to consider scheduling a vacation, adventure of sorts, or of course anything which expands their horizons. The individual would be more keen and interested towards higher and deeper learning of life in its full spectrum and the person should be cautious during this time of transit not to overlook the daily routine duties and responsibilities.

Sun Transits the Tenth House

This is the time when the individual's focus would be drawn to his/her career, profession, business or standing in the society or external world and reputation. During this time the person would be more interested and focussed on achieving something in life. His/her actions would be result oriented and would be quite practical in every sense. The person will be in limelight either on a small or large scale as per his/her normal course of life. He/she may be entrusted with some important work, project etc. to undertake to prove his/her worth. And rightly so, the individual would have good chance of achieving something credible and make a name in the professional and social circles and the added responsibilities which come along with the recognition.

Sun Transits the Eleventh House

This period would be a period of co-operation with other people. Engaging in group efforts and projects in the individual's personal and professional life, which will be the most effective way to accomplish the objectives and goals. The person should be social and study the people around him/her and thus there would be some gains through friends and elders. This time of transit would be a time for team work in all spheres. During this transit the individual could enjoy new position, honour, gain of money, happiness. There could be success and prosperity in undertakings, good food, domestic bliss, recovery from any health issues and good health, may help and uplift the under privileged and also perform some good deeds and could eventually gain.

Sun Transits the Twelfth House

During this time of transit the individual would analyse thoroughly all his/her actions, thoughts, relationships etc., as this could be a time of some deep introspection and corrections required, wherever. There could be some uncertainties which could turn out suddenly. Situations that would have naturally outgrown their usefulness in the individual's life can now be put behind and move forward in life with new energy and outlook.

Chapter 10

Transit of Moon

Transit of Moon through houses lasts for 2 days and 6 hours in each house and is quite significance during the transit. Natal Moon is one of the most powerful point in the individual's horoscope, the effects would be felt for couple of hours. But in case of major change of phase such as new Moon or full Moon upon a natal planet, the influence remains for one to four weeks. The effects of Eclipse on a natal planet may felt for several months. The effects generally are change of moods, transient, encounter with others, and passing feelings. Most important of Moon's signification is that of mind, and everything achievable, whether positive or negative starts in mind first before physically getting manifested. Thus the thinking style, thinking process could get affected during Moon's transit.

Transit of Moon through houses indicates the areas of the person's life to which he/she should turn his/her greatest attention. To check a particular day, transit of Moon is of utmost importance.

Moon Transits the First House

Transit of Moon in first house generally indicates good health, increase in gains, good food, mental and sensual comforts, sexual enjoyments and new clothes. Good fortune, pleasant meetings with friends etc. as the individual would be emotionally warm for persons around him/her and can be emotionally demanding as well. But control and caution is also advised during this period. It's a good time to focus on new beginnings and fresh starts. During this time the individual is more sensitive to the vibrations and energies around themselves, particularly in their immediate environment. The person is inclined to act on impulse, or to react automatically based on his/her basic emotional orientation, rather than approaching the world objectively, which calls for a cautious approach. It's easy to be emotionally touched by something during this period, and also to feel hurt or disappointed. In the 2-1/4 days of this transit one tends to take things quite personally. Some restlessness is likely during this time, and could force the individual to make some small personal changes, such as changing one's 'look' or their living environment in small ways. The person might deal with society and public in a different way because of the Moon's effect on emotions and one could also be feeling emotional or sensitive about one's appearance or manners.

Moon Transits the Second House

During this transit of over 2 days there could be some ordinary gain of money but the same time it could indicate some mental tension, conflicts with family or friends, obstacles in undertakings, expenditure and disputes. Strong attachment to material objects could get developed. The individual needs to be careful against lending money to someone as the chances of getting it back could be lesser if lent during this period. Excess expenditures are best avoided during this time. The individual would focus on emotional security. New experiences are best avoided during this time and as far as possible status quo should be maintained.

Moon Transits the Third House

During this transit of over 2 days marks one of the busier periods in the lunar month and activities may be centred around making errands, short trips, calls, and other communication. Mentally the individual would tend to be restless, easily bored, and could be in need of stimulation. The person may find it hard to focus on any one particular task and his/her curiosity would get ignited. New friendships or contacts might be made. You might find yourself talking more than usual, perhaps about the past. Emotional communications could get figured during this period. This period indicates Success, gain of good dresses, friendship, and association with opposite sex, gain of money, victory in some ventures, joy and happiness. Communication and personal conversation would have an emotional depth and will be fruitful. Thus control of emotions will be helpful. Third house is house of e very day world, the transit indicates bad impression upon some one by reacting spontaneously rather than, thinking and reacting cautiously which would save the day. Relatives and friends may play an important role in the person's life during this time.

Moon Transits the Fourth House

During this transit of over 2 days, the individual's attention turns inward and towards his/her domestic affairs. They would feel the need for more privacy than usual, and may tend to focus on building or solidifying their domestic base. They will have a greater need for security and the feeling of being safe and comfortable during this period. This is a time for building one's sense of security. Family and personal matters take precedence over worldly affairs during this transit. The way the individual handles his domestic support system at this stage in his/her life would determine their mood. A good time to relax at home and avoid any sorts of confrontation or conflict situation. He/she will feel emotionally more possessive both to things and intimate relationships, they need to be cautious else, they could lose the things they would be holding on. This transit time one should adopt a free attitude for success. If the individual is careless and gets in to controversies and conflicts this transit could create suspicion of everybody and everything, fear, trouble, sorrows, loss of money, mental worry and domestic unhappiness. Also they need to keep an eye on their health.

Moon Transits the Fifth House

During this transit of over two days the individual could be more outgoing than the previous few days of the Moon's transit of the fourth house. This duration would be an expressive time for the person and his/her energies would be directed outwards as they feel more confident moving about in the outside world. They will have an emotional need to be heard, seen, and noticed. An increased desire to create, and to display their talents, is often experienced during this phase. Recreation, hobbies, romance, and anything that gives pleasure is now more important to them than usual. The individual would feel especially amorous or more inclined to express the feelings of love during this time. Relatives and friends may tend to tune into the person emotionally. There could be a sudden desire to see a movie, explore a creative urge, play a game, or take part in a play, etc. during this period. Enjoyment would be theme during this period. In love affairs, the person will experience greater emotional depth than usual and his/her experience with their lover will be much more intense. The person should not be possessive of the other person they love but should give due regard to other's feeling also. Relations with children or a loved one would be better. In addition, they could experience increased expenditure, illness, indigestion and some short journeys.

Moon Transits the Sixth House

This transit of Moon for over 2 days through the sixth house of the natal chart Indicates a need and/or desire to perfect one's profession. This is a time of dedication to work, health, and routine. This is a more Introverted period during which one might have to work hard and keep abreast of everything, that is a sheer hard work phase. The individual might set his/her feelings aside in order to learn and take care of details of their work. Their senses would be more acute and they could find minor aches and pains would be more noticeable and also, they could find that little things that are out of order in their lives become more apparent. Cleaning and re-organizing may be in order during this transit. Their mood is likely to impact their health more than ever thus, they should try not to stress over little things. Instead, work on improving and perfecting the smaller systems in their life so thot they can move on comfortably. This period also indicates gain of wealth joy, overpowering enemies, good health and friends, happiness and acquisition of desired objects. Holding back unpleasant emotions of one kind or another is a probable attribute of this transit. The individual should pay attention to home, personal hygiene, and organisation of personal aspects of life. Finally one should take care of their health which is essential.

Moon Transits the Seventh House

During the transit of Moon in one's seventh house of the natal chart, close personal and business relationships could be the highlight. The relationships or partnerships would be largely determined by the individual's moods during this transit period and he/she might have emotional confrontations during this time or warm, nurturing relations, again depending on their current circumstances. Sometimes this transit correlates with the need for a discussion or a consultation with personal relationship matters. An increased need to be with people, to socialize, and to compromise could also be the feature during this transit. More attention to physical appearance and attractiveness, as well as graciousness, could also figure. The person would be in a position to learn much about themselves by listening to others. The need to create or maintain a harmonious environment dominates at this time but getting to that point can entail some delays. Feeling emotional about one's relationships could also figure out during this transit time. This transit is also a good time for finding a life partner or getting the marriage fixed or getting married.

Moon Transits the Eighth House

During this transit of Moon there can be a desire which gets generated for acquiring some insights in to deeper experiences and more powerful bonds. Emotional commitments come into focus during this period of transit. The individual would be looking for more meaning in his/her life, and any activity that stirs their emotions gets attracted. On a more ground level, money and possessions could be emotional issues now. It would be beneficial to know that one could over-react to matters during this transit, finding it hard to detach oneself emotionally in order to look at life objectively. The person may not be too sociable during this brief period and may prefer to analyse everything including even relationships. Some untoward events may get experienced during this time such as, fear of loss of money, anger, ill health, some minor conflicts, anxiety etc.

Moon Transits the Ninth House

Freedom on all levels would be the focus during this 2 and half days' transit, when not only physical freedom of movement and expression, but mental and spiritual freedom as well would take the precedence. The emotional need during this time will be, expansion and growth. The person may not want to be limited by boundaries or barriers. This placement of the Moon indicates inclination to be more sociable and amenable to friends and family. Independence, new experiences, and intellectual growth would be the major focus. The person may tend to take more trips or embark on adventures, big or small during this transit as emotional boredom or restlessness could be at the root of this behaviour, where breaking the routine will be in order. This will be a good time to catch a break and get some perspective on one's life. Feeling emotional about one's opinions or beliefs could also come up in one's life during this transit. The individual may feel like deviating from daily routine and do it, because travel could feel beneficial to overcome his/her boredom for a short period. He/she may meet new friends from a foreign country or from a distant place. This will cause

Fatigue and unexpected expenses and some health issues such as digestive or stomach disorders etc.

Moon Transits the Tenth House

The individual's attention during this transit would be on approval and recognition. The focus would be on establishing some sort of order and control in their life. There would be a stronger need for recognition and for concrete success. Discontent with one's position in life could be magnified during this period. Matters surrounding one's profession or the authority figures in one's life come to the foreground. Sensitivity to the person's reputation or how others view them can figured out during this time. He/she would be noticed for what they do and don't do, similarly for what they have done or haven't done. This transit is the time to be on one's best behaviour. Other aspects of this transit could be achievement of desired objects, position of command, success, pleasure, happiness and comforts at home. Receipt of gifts and presents. There could be success in business and professional pursuits. The person would be at his/her best efficiency during this transit to be able to display their talents and may succeed to get a good position in their professional career and can win over others. A good transit for any kind of public relations work or sale of property. The individual could also get long overdue recognition during this transit.

Moon Transits the Eleventh House

This transit of the Moon is a more sociable and amenable period for the individual. Stronger social awareness and a desire to belong to a group may be the thought-process during this period, although sometimes it's more about expressing his/her own individuality and going against the rules. Networking and making new friendships and contacts would be the main theme during this period of over two days. It's a good time to spend with friends or known social-groups. However, the individual would be more sensitive to the moods of those around him/her, and they could feel being emotional about their sense of belonging or distance with the like-minded people. In friendships they will feel more protective and supportive than usual or attract others for emotional reasons, and they would convey their emotions and sentiments openly to their friends whatever they could not convey earlier as the contacts would be much deeper during this period. A related effect of this transit is to bring friend or friends of opposite sex into prominence in their life, and in general will be easy to get along with them. They may also be excessively possessive of a friend. This transit period could also be helpful in establishing contacts with long last friends.

Moon Transits the Twelfth House

The individual would have heightened sensitivity and an emotional need to connect with the inner world that is the philosophical, spiritual and related domains, such approach would be there and dominant during this transit. This is often a more introverted period when the focus is on the dreams and desires, personal creativity, and sensitivity. Time spent alone may be necessary, and some form of emotional retreat is natural. The person would be more insecure than usual, and it would be prudent to hold back on starting new projects for the time being. There could be aspects such as dependence, laziness jealousy, loss, expenditure, injury or accident and misunderstanding with friends and relatives. The person might also have secretive mind to keep one's feelings, so he/she need to communicate their deep inner feelings to another person whom they can trust. Relations with the opposite sex will be difficult and erratic. The individual may prefer to be left alone. A good transit for getting involved in mystical or spiritual discipline.

Chapter 11

Transit of Mercury

Transit of Mercury is important to study, this transit in the horoscope indicates shifts of mental focus and attention with respect to the attributes of the houses and planets it transits. The kind of communications the individual would have with other people, also an indicator of travel, and short trips in every day routine. Mercury signifies communications received as well as sent, during this transit. The person may receive many letters, telephone calls and unexpected visits. Rational mind is also ruled by Mercury and gives clarity of ideas and thoughts, if Mercury is not afflicted during transit and in birth horoscope. Events which begin when Mercury is retrograde could end or get modified or changed suddenly and may also terminate unexpectedly or do not indicate all that is expected. Mercury indicates good results in 2nd, 4th, 6th, 8th 10th and 11th houses provided their corresponding Vedha places namely 5th, 3rd, 9th, 1st, 8th and 12th houses are not occupied by any of the planet other than Moon. Mercury transits in a sign or house for about a month.

Mercury Transits the First House

This transit duration is a period in which the person would be inclined to speak up about matters that he/she previously were only mulling over. Their disposition would be more intellectual than usual during this period, and self-expression comes easy. They will be sharper than usual and more observant, and more inclined to listen. Relationships with siblings, neighbours, and friends may become more prominent in their life during this transit period. It is likely that the person will initiate discussions during this period, evaluate their appearance and the impact they have on those around them, and make contact with others rather than stay chained to any one place or activity. This is the time to be direct and to communicate their needs and Interests. They would be more inclined to talk about themselves and their personal past during this period and this is where care needs to be taken. This may also be a restless time when it could be difficult to turn the thinking process off when it would be better to relax. This transit is an especially fruitful time for any endeavour that requires dealing with words, ideas, and facts and figures. The individual's demeanour would be more youthful, perhaps mischievous, light hearted, and non-threatening because of which others might be more inclined to turn to this person for advice or pleasant conversation. Using the power of words to attract what the person wants or to further her/his interests works best for the person during this time. A good time to express one's views and examine oneself. Her/his mind will be more active, they would not be deceptive, and they will not change their view point often and try to control it. In case Mercury is afflicted in birth chart or in transit in this house, the person may feel nervousness and anxiety, and may get involved in some mental problem. They should try to relax and remain away from serious thoughts.

Short travels are indicated which could be beneficial. An afflicted Mercury indicates affect from enemies, loss of some money, some kind of fear, hurtful speech, unsteady mind, change of opinion by force and company of unwanted persons.

Mercury Transits the Second House

This is a strong period for analysing one's cash flow, income, and earning power. The individual would be more practical and rational in her/his approach to finances during this period. With one's conscious mind focused on money and possessions, as well as personal values, this can be a strong period for gathering new money or wealth generating ideas. Alternatively, it could be a time when the person tends to ponder over his/her finances. Conversations tend to be practical rather than frivolous during this transit period. Financial gain may come through communications. The individual would tend to think in the right direction with respect to material, intellectual or spiritual side. She/he may enter into negotiations with others regarding money or property including professional career, business and its progress or expansion. In case of affliction of Mercury either in the natal chart or during this transit one should avoid financial or property deals during this time. His/her mind could become clouded and may get misled by other persons.

This transit will have the power to generate additional income and gain of money, reliable friends, good food, success in undertakings but it could also indicate some insults, scandals and unjust blames etc. if Mercury is afflicted.

Mercury Transits the Third House

In the third house Mercury is in its home, and offers a natural curiosity, facility with words, and the ability to multi-task successfully. More time spent on communicating and writing, making short frequent trips, chatting, running errands, communicating with friends, siblings, colleagues, visiting friends and relatives, and doing paperwork is likely during this transit period. There can also be a tendency to ponder over insignificant matters during this time. Also, and overdose of information is a possibility during this time. The individual's interests are especially varied at this time and perhaps scattered. This would be an ideal time to pick up information from one's environment and the people in it, as the person's tendency would be towards a certain level of intellectual detachment during this time. The mind could get distracted often, particularly when circumstances call for the individual to stick to routine, so this would be the time when the person should be extra careful in taking up even routine tasks. The mind would be especially inquisitive during this cycle, when learning, or during short trips, and other forms of communication and making connections, appeal strongly, and some persons could be quite fidgety or nervous during this cycle, perhaps due to increased errands, excessive communication and the challenge of tackling a variety of subjects. Talking to near and dear ones, writing, and studying can be good ways to handle stress. This transit also indicates group discussions and conversations with others, meet new people, travel, contact with relatives and new people. A favourable time for intellectual works. This is not an ideal time to relax as it can create some sort of fear of losing things because of either no-action or no-communication. This transit time should be used to get information first and then to act on it as required. In entering into contracts, business partnerships, dealing with others, the person should be wise enough to postpone and plan it to do in the next house transit of Mercury in the fourth house. The individual should also avoid binding his/her point of view on others.

Mercury Transits the Fourth House

This transit is a time during which one can enjoy increased powers of concentration. The person would perform better if he/she gets solitude in order to get mental work done during this cycle. Their memory will be better and will have increased retentive power than during normal times and, their thoughts often turn to personal matters, family, and loved ones. The person might particularly enjoy discussions about themselves, their past, or family matters during this transit. This period is a good time to open up conversations with loved ones, friends and others on important matters, as the person would be more rational when it comes to understanding things in their right perspective. Their mind could often wander on domestic concerns and issues surrounding your home, family, property, conveyances and personal past. This transit sometimes indicates an especially busy, and perhaps hectic, period on the domestic scene. For example, the person might take home professional work or find that people drop by their home often during this cycle for some work. This transit indicates fulfilment of their plans, schemes and contracts etc. for gain of money and enjoyment. Other indications of this transit are prosperity to relations and family, happiness, contacts with good persons, domestic happiness and own prosperity. Family matters could get settled during this time. Communications will be gainful.

Mercury Transits the Fifth House

During this transit period there could be a strong mental connection with one's creative side. The person would have intelligent ideas and thoughts and will be quite good at expressing them to others smoothly. Their thinking will be more creative than usual and they will tend to entertain others with their conversation end their sense of humour also would be strong. The individual would be beneficial to children in various ways, there could also be pleasures or romance during this expressive transit. He/she might enjoy researching speculative ventures during this time and could also enjoy games that involve competing with others on mental level. They will have a stronger need for intellectual stimulation and thus the person could appreciate friends and partner if they are intellectual type of individuals The person would be more willing to take risks on a mental level during this time thus he/she would tend to take advantage of the increased spontaneity and creativity that comes during this transit. In case of affliction, the person may also experience loss of position or of money, aimless undertakings, some loss on personality front, and disharmony in domestic surroundings.

Mercury Transits the Sixth House

This is a good placement for Mercury, as it is the natural ruler of the sixth house, especially if Mercury is a functional benefic for the individual's chart. This would be a good period for sorting out the details of one's daily existence as he/she would be mostly involved in paying bills or clearing out their debts and sort out clutter, and take up some detailed and minute work. Health matters will be most certainly on one's mind, and he/she could be thinking of scheduling check-ups or busy researching ways to improve their health. They may also show interest in improving their base skills. The person's approach to work during this transit will be pleasant, happy, and logical for the most part unless he/she allows worry or scattered energy to enter the picture. The person will be inclined to learn new work skills, or to improve his/her skills and output in terms of work. There is likely to be more activity, movement, contact and communications with co-workers during this transit. The person would tend to take more Interest In organising working environment and handle the routine and dally affairs and all of the little things that contribute to efficiency and competency.

Menial tasks become more prominent. The individual however should watch out things which would interfere with work output during this transit. Health and work are signified by the sixth house. This is a good time for mental work to gain success and popularity, planning one's projects carefully for benefits. Mental and domestic happiness would be there. Will have good relation with superiors and subordinates during this transit thus can build upon the relationships further. Affliction to this house or to Mercury can indicate some issues with health related to nervous system etc. and the person may feel nervous or anxious to strain the body which should be avoided. Care for the diet is a must.

Mercury Transits the Seventh House

During this transit the person would tend to weigh the pros and cons of every issue which he/she comes across taking into account others' needs as well as their own. They could be having a tough time being able to take decisive actions, as they would be inclined to see all points of view which could delay their decisions. They will have a strong desire to cooperate and communicate with others at this time and they will feel quite comfortable spending time with people on an individual level rather than in groups, or with those with whom they share a personal history. Their own thoughts become clearer through dialogue with others. The person could be engaged in public relations work, counselling, negotiating, or arbitration during this transit. There will be a lot of emphasis on communications with partners and best friends at this time and they can use the power of words to advise others or to make peace with people in their life. They will be more diplomatic than usual during this transit and also they will be able to explain any issue in detail to their partner, spouse or family to avoid mental worry etc. They would not think or act alone but try to take help of others. Communication is the central key objective during this transit which needs to be utilised properly and with smartness to tide over any matter such as, domestic worries, disagreement with close relations, friends etc. Arguments and controversies are best avoided especially during this time. He/she can enter into negotiations, contracts about any matter, if Mercury is not afflicted, else such things are best postponed.

Mercury Transits the Eighth House

During this transit period the individual would be more intuitive than usual, picking up all of the hidden cues from people around themselves and will also be good in reading between the lines. This is a good time during which one can undertake some financial planning. Research would also be favourable during this time. The

person can utilise this period to approach sensitive, intimate, and personal matters with rationality and logic. As
such, this will be a good time to open up conversations about topics that normally might cause flutters, such as those connected to sharing of power, intimacy and finances. One can look forward to cheerfulness, steadiness, and victory over opponents. The person would be generally happy and will have good intellect and authority. One can ponder over their hidden aspects. Deep thinking and action will pay the person more than usual but they should not get carried away by fantasy and thoughts. Finance and property dealings may be good to be undertaken during this time which could turn out profitable.

Mercury Transits the Ninth House

During this transit the individual may not like to focus on routine things, and would be more interested in practical matters, and they would look for bigger visions, thoughts, and ideals. They will be open to expanding their knowledge base during this cycle, and communications from or with someone. They will be putting everything into perspective now, rather than restricting themselves to a limited exposure. They will be more inclined to discuss broader philosophies during this time. He/she will be inclined during this transit to think about the big picture rather than the routine things and details of their life. Missing appointments and other forms of forgetfulness could be part of the picture at this time. This is also a good time for studying subjects relating to foreign places, law, philosophy or higher knowledge of any type would be beneficial. The individual may have dealings with officials of law or those in position of authority. This is a good time for travel, conversation and communication with others.

Mercury Transits the Tenth House

During this transit the individual will focus on his/her career and business matters. Also, the profession would require more than usual communication during this time. You speak with authority during this period, and he/she would be more accountable than usual for what they communicate. Their Ideas may come into public view during this time. They may also use the power of words either written or verbal, to influence authority figures. This is an excellent period for developing career and professional plans or strategies. They may get approached by others for advice or for their expert or specialist opinion on important matters. Although approachable and ready to communicate, this person would be less inclined towards chatting about frivolous matters during this transit period. The person may tend to think about his/her position or standing on a professional level more frequently during this transit. They will be likely doing some multi-tasking regarding career and business matters. If Mercury is afflicted either in the natal chart or if there is a Vedha to this transit, its influence would be to worry unnecessarily about their reputation and responsibilities. Good health, gain of money and increased income, success in profession, enjoyment, all round success, mental and domestic happiness, success over opponents and property are the attributes of this transit if Mercury is benefic both in the natal chart as well as in this transit. A Good period for profession during which one may make plans for making changes, to talk to superiors about the progress of work for getting better place or promotion, which would also depend on birth chart but surely a way to go about improving ones career. The individual may undertake studies of new subjects. Communications will be generally gainful with the outside world, through advertising, contracts or negotiations, especially if there is no afflicted planet in tenth house in the chart and is not being transited by another planet at the same time.

Mercury Transits the Eleventh House

The individual's thinking capacity would be very good during this transit and his/her mind will be bright, alert, and active during this period, and they will have the ability to come up with unusual and inventive ideas. Sharing their thoughts with others would be of interest to this person and they would be in an advantageous position. Others will tend to particularly enjoy their conversations during this transit, as the person would be willing to listen as well as add their own thoughts. Also, their ability to grasp unusual subject matter and to intuitively understand what others try to say will win hearts and minds. They will also do a lot of thinking and musing about their own happiness and long-term goals. This is a time of increased communications and social interactions and discourses. They may develop new friendships with youngsters and they will be happy at home, would gain some prosperity, money. Some honour and satisfaction out of their achievements could come up during this time as this would be a good and favourable time. Group working will be beneficial as will be some intellectual exchanges with friends and colleagues. If Mercury is benefic in the natal chart and if there is no Vedha in this transit, the individual could benefit immensely with respect to gains.

Mercury Transits the Twelfth House

During this transit period the individual could deal with some confidential and secret information. People opposed to him/her could raise some unwanted issues which he/she may have to deal with it, thus a much careful approach in all matters is advisable during this time. The individual needs to be quite smart in utilising and handling confidential information and things will work out well. Spiritual and religious matters with increased ability and research will be an extraordinary good point of this transit. Heavy expenditure and loss of money could also be felt if things are overlooked. The individual could be focused on private matters and past Issues during this period. During this transit the person may be less likely to speak or communicate freely about what they think on various issues. This is a good time for research, quiet contemplation, and meditation, but one should avoid being dragged down by issues that would have outgrown their worth and purpose. Examining the past in order to improve the future is certainly worthwhile, as long as no energies are wasted on futile matters. Creative endeavours could prosper during this time particularly those that draw upon the emotions or that require creative visualization skills, such as poetry, art, acting, and other such activities. One would likely require a certain amount of solitude in order to get his/her thoughts together or to be mentally productive. They will be less likely to chat indiscriminately during this transit, and tend to be a little secretive or tight-lipped for the time being. This may be important, in fact, because this position is sometimes associated with uncovering of secrets, so discretion may be in order.

Chapter 12

Transit of Mars

Mars during its transit in 3rd, 6th and 11th houses from natal Moon indicates positive and beneficial effects if the 12th, 5th, and 9th places respectively are free from transit of other planets at that time that is no Vedhas are present. Mars transits in a sign for around 45 days. In other houses traditionally it is considered a malefic planet or the one indicating negative effects but this phenomenon is generally misunderstood, the reason being Mars indicates energy and an individual might either lack in energy or may have excessive energy or normal levels of energy as per the factual position of Mars in the natal chart, Dashas and transits and related Vedhas. The energy levels may be either lesser or more than the required limits, thus making the individual behave in a different way than he/she should. If the energies as indicated by Mars are allowed to operate to excess, its effects then can be quite difficult to handle, which might give rise to negative situations, thus the 'malefic' indications coming to play.

But usually this should not be taken as a setback and instead ways and means should be explored to utilise energies manifesting as either emotions, sentiments, anger, anxiety etc. as all these are part and parcel of life. The energy is used to maintain himself/herself in the face of pressures from world environments to maintain their position. Persons with weak energy levels may find it quite difficult to go through the grinding routines and activities of life, thus it is quite necessary that position of Mars in the birth chart should be strong. Persons with strong Mars generally dominate others. Its transit indicates energy and vigour. In fact one way to ensure that transit of Mars doesn't indicate disputes or arguments with others depends on the sign of transit and the person needs to work hard to cope with various situations. It being a fiery planet, indicates rashness, hot temper, accidents, cuts, wounds, operation etc.

Mars when transits over Venus or a sign of Venus, the person seeks out physical love. When over Mercury, one looks for mental activity. In short when Mars transits a planet, the effects of that planet are ignited through the energy of Mars. The person will try to establish his/her individuality towards others through the issues related to that planet/sign. When Mars transits a house, either synergy or conflicts with others in the areas of your life could arise. The high energy levels of Mars at physical level indicate accidents, especially from burns or fire, and illness involving fever, high blood pressure and infection etc.

Mars Transits the First House

This transit period is a time to make impression upon others with much activity with hard work. Every relationship could be difficult to manage but working independently will pay the person more than usual. The person would be dominant during this transit more than the usual. Care should be taken during this transit that the individual should not get in to arguments, conflicts and/or fights. He/she should be careful against illness, injuries due to accidents, falls etc. during the period of this period of transit. The person would will feel dejected, and may also find obstacles in tasks and daily activities, displeasure of superiors. They should take care of health against any blood related infections. One of the indications, if Mars is afflicted in the natal chart is, this transit may indicate separation of relations and friends. The person would be able to stand his/her ground and assert themselves more than the usual during this transit as they will have good energy levels at their disposal to take their plans ahead, and these individuals will be more enterprising as they want to leave their mark on the world in some way however big or small, They will be able to make a good impression on others whom they come across. If circumstances force them, they will able to easily fight back and also may be somewhat combative under the influence of this transit and may have a short temper, thus it will be better to avoid being aggressive. The individual will take charge of life, and at the same time may also have a lasting impression on others because of their approach. This is an excellent transit for assertiveness and physical vitality.

Love affairs may also get stepped up during this period.

Mars Transits the Second House

The second house represents, food, speech, finance, family, length of life, wealth etc. The person during this transit will be quite concerned with his/her financial matters and as far as possible attempts and control should be exerted not to go overboard with the concerns. Another characteristic of this transit would be to involve the individual in matters pertaining to some family matters which would keep them occupied even for very trivial reason as getting entangled in conflicts and disputes is possible during this transit period thus a more carefree approach would always help in keeping matters in the right perspective. There could be some positive progress in property matters if Mars is benefic in the natal chart and if there are no Vedhas during this transit. The individual could become slightly more possessive in nature during this transit to counter the wasteful expenditure indicated during this time.

On the positive side, one's efforts will be to complete a work, and will use all the influences. There could be some displeasure of superiors and of those in power and authority. The person should take care against thefts even if minor during this period. Harsh temperament, anxiety, increased expenditure, disputes etc. can also not be ruled out especially with malefic natal Mars. The person will have more energy at her/his disposal not just to make money, but also to defend their values. This can be a very resourceful time, when one makes the most of what they have. They will have good levels of energy for taking up new ventures, projects and tasks which would generate additional finances along with stepping up existing ones. The person may be mentally quite focussed on protecting his/her possessions and also could be trying to prove themselves in their field to others. If conflicts occur during this transit, they are likely to be over issues of ownership of anything. This is a time when impulse buying is could be at a peak which should be controlled. The person should avoid using credit during this transit duration as their spending habits may be excessive and impulsive.

Mars Transits the Third House

During this transit the individual is likely to have many ideas and plans going during this transit and he/she might be inclined to pass on their energy. This is a good time to inform others about their strengths and ideas or to present their case. They may also be especially busy running errands and communicating with others. During this transit duration the person would be more disciplined, and presentable and may also have an assertive communication style at this time. It is possible that circumstances may get heated, or they may escalate into arguments, thus care should be taken not to over indulge in discussions. There could be a tendency to be impatient or impulsive while driving or while performing manual tasks, generally with the hands, which in turn may lead to injuries or accidents, thus it's wise to be careful during performing any activity such as driving, while operating machinery or simply using scissors, knives etc. This is a good time to work on intellectual tasks with more vigour and passion. The energies will be high, and at the same time there is considerable chance of conflicts with persons of daily contact, friends, neighbours or relatives. The person could be argumentative and disagreement with others with one's views should not be taken as a personal affront. The individual should not coerce others. This is a good period for expressing oneself through ideas, mails etc.

A good period for any kind of vigorous mental work. On the whole, the person will enjoy good health, happiness, gain of money, all-round success, strength, good position, honour, authority and pleasure from children as well as partner.

Mars Transits the Fourth House

The person will have more energy at his/her disposal for domestic projects or
Activities during this transit duration. Their actions are governed more by instincts during this period and they may be especially defensive and protective and could work hard at making themselves feel more secure, and they may also be called upon to take charge on the home and family front. They will have more energy and inclination to invest in domestic matters even if trivial in nature as house repairs, aesthetics or other domestic chores. If they feel quite restless, moody, or defensive during this period, it would be a good idea to take up any of the domestic activities or tasks. They may also have an increased desire to rule over all matters and if this transit stimulates conflict or disputes, it is likely to be related to home, family or relationships. There is a chance the person could get in to arguments with those people who would be close to him/her and may also encounter opposition from career-related matters or people. The individual would get worked up about old matters or emotional issues from the past that could resurface during this transit duration. At home one should contend with others and if they don't agree with them

there could be chances of disturbances of homely bliss during this transit.

In various situations, one would behave in a compulsive manner which may aggravate the situation resulting in the situation not so favourable. Relationships would be difficult to maintain during this transit due to various commitments and there may be some opposition in professional life which will make this time even more tedious to manage. Thus it is advisable for the individual to keep his/her emotions, anger, and anxiety under control during this transit for maintaining domestic bliss and peace. To sum up during this transit, one may experience domestic issues and misunderstandings, professional difficulties and some issues due to opponents.

Mars Transits the Fifth House

Mars transit in the fifth house time is self-expressive time when the person has lots of energy, but not necessarily self-discipline to match the energy level and he/she has more energy at his/her disposal to express themselves creatively, through activities which could have some depth in their meaning and outcome. They may also get involved in romantic encounters, hobbies which they are passionate about, or sports. Their love life may get prominent and centre of focus as this could be an especially passionate time. The individual would tend to put more energy into play and pleasure and at the same time they need to be careful not to burn the candle at both ends. Also, they need to watch out for a tendency to speculate or gamble as these could lead to sure-shot losses. They will be more playful than usual, and especially magnetic. This transit period would give a egoistic mind-set. Being a house of pleasure, any game and sports activities could get rewarded more so as Mars also represents sports. Physical contacts will tend increase with friends, acquaintances and especially with opposite sex. Children may not have serious conflict with the person and the person could find situation harder to handle. They need to keep themselves busy and also be careful against any accidents and injuries. Thus they need to be cautious of improper desires, mental anguish trouble and quarrels with children, wounds or injuries through accidents, physical weakness, theft of belongings and irritable temperament etc.

Mars Transits the Sixth House

The individual will have good energy levels for every work and daily routines tend to get speeded up during this transit. The person could have a larger workload than usual. It's a great lime to take charge of one's health as the person has good levels of reserve energy at their disposal which they can utilise to pick up health and physical activity related regimen. It might be easy for the individual to work with others in a harmonious manner during this transit and disputes and misunderstandings with co-workers will be at minimum. It would be wise to find little projects and things to do so that they can channelise their energy constructively. If health gets affected with fevers or infections, recovery could be quicker during this period. They can utilise this transit duration to get their pending works completed and getting things done. Sixth house also indicates service and credit for the work done.

The person should avoid conflicts and arguments over disagreements with seniors and colleagues during this time. There could be chances for proving their worth in professional career. The transit also indicates happiness,, success in tough ventures, overcoming difficulties and litigations, gain, honour, prosperity. Favour from superiors can also be expected, comforts, increased income etc. Care for good health would be needed.

Mars Transits the Seventh House

During this transit of Mars, partnerships may get effected and there could be some conflicts, or the individual may get challenged by some adversaries. The person needs to be quite diplomatic and use all the wit and tact to get around the tricky situations which could arise during this time. There could be some issues in relationships and friendships. The person may seem to need someone's help in order to do what he/she wants to do during this time. Relationship matters would be dynamic during this period. When a difference arises, the person would be quick to settle it and also they will have little patience for delaying things for resolving them at a later time, instead they will go all out to resolve pending matters. Their close personal relationships will be lively during this transit duration and may get involved in some resolutions or reconciliation. A tension in life is indicated during this transit, which can be overcome by co-operating with partners, friends, life-partner and/or colleagues. Some unknown opponents may try to create some disturbances. The individual may find it difficult to give in and compromise in marriage, partnership etc. also they should try to avoid unnecessary conflicts with others, legal proceedings, and law suits etc. and hence try to compromise if they can, in order to avoid controversies and conflicts. The positive side of the transit could be too much compromise and clearing the grievances between them and their life-partner, business-partners or other close friends. They can make adjustments during this period for smooth relations. The negative side denotes quarrels with partners, indigestion, loss of some money, disputes with friends and partners, mental agony and anxiety etc.

Mars Transits the Eighth House

During this transit sexuality, sensual pleasures and intimacy get stimulated, thus the individual could come across opposite sex partners or friends. Also during this transit there could be triggers for extra-marital relationships which the person should guard against. Mars transit of the eighth house indicates energies in such a way that a tendency towards ego conflicts concerning money matters, property or some wealth issues could prop up during this time. Conflicts with partners over values or possessions are possible. Occasionally, this transit could bring a crisis or an abrupt closure of matters of some kind. Something which comes to the knowledge during this time will have the potential to disturb or touch the person deeply. The individual would be likely to be more strategic in her/his actions during this period, as they become aware of the subtleties of human interaction. This is a time when the person's best course of action is to recognise that they need, or rely on, others for support. Mars here can indicate some health issues as well, such as fever, injuries due to accidents, loss of money, blood related health issues, mental worries and fatigue etc. The effects can be either subtle or blatant. There could be confrontation with others due to some ego issues. Eighth house being the house of values that one shares with others, this transit may also indicate powerful effects in him/her which may be cause for a change in the individual.

There could be some disagreements or conflicts with the life-partner. This transit would not be a good time to raise a loan from anybody. This transit may transform the individual by changing the way he/she thinks.

Mars Transits the Ninth House

The individual can perform more creative and intellectual work than usual during this transit duration of Mars. There would be influence over others for good impression but the person should not be dogmatic in his/her opinion, thus they should avoid forcing down their ideas and thoughts about religion, philosophy and other important areas in life, on others. Expansion in their sphere of influence and professional matters would be quite likely which would prove good. If possible they may avoid long distance travels during this period and if that is not possible they should be quite careful through their travel period. Ninth house is the house of law and the courts, thus under certain circumstances this transit can indicate legal issues which could get well settled if natal Mars is benefic and if there are no Vedhas to Mars during this transit else there could be some hurdles in getting the issues settled and which could result in mental anxiety, wearisome journeys, humiliations, some losses etc. During this period, one would be especially enthusiastic, bold and more energetic than usual. Some restlessness and hunger for adventure would be experienced during this period. The person would be looking to expand her/his activities, and may find that they have a lot of energy for higher studies, travel, or simply understanding new subjects. Negative potentials include having strong opinions on various issues or getting easily fired up and excited over differences in points of view, or legal tussles.

Mars Transits the Tenth House

During this transit the individual could face some hurdles and blockages in her/his business or professional career and there could be some health matters which may require rest. This time may also indicate anxiety about profession but during the same transit, in the second half period of transit the person could have good effects. The person needs to be careful and recognise the needs of others. The person could achieve big things during this period with sincere hard work and efforts. As far as possible frictions, arguments should be avoided during this transit as that will have the potential to get aggravated which may create some hurdles in the advancement in work related matters. They should be conscious of other's interests and try to understanding their point of view as well.

This transit stimulates the ambition and/or the desire to be recognised for accomplishments. Whether it's professional or personal, the person is likely to have an increased desire for others to notice his/her achievements. This can be a good time to become self-employed or start a business if other factors are favourable and if Mars is benefic in the natal chart. The person would try her/his best to pour more energy into self-promotion activities or business or career related activities.

Mars Transits the Eleventh House

This transit of mars in to a house of group relationship which indicates success by working in a conducive manner along with the team. Thus the person should try and cooperate with all his/her colleagues. Team work is the catch word during this transit of Mars in the eleventh house and try to maintain balance every-where for success. They could gain some additional money from some quarters during this transit. People connected to sports will have good progress during this time and will be beneficial and rewarding for their hard work and may also get some recognition and awards. Overall the person can have financial gain, good health, happiness and enjoyment, profits from business or properties, may acquire some material luxuries, could get success in undertakings etc. Group activities and cooperative efforts are the best way to achieve goals during this time. The person should avoid allowing the ego to attempt to dominate others. They may prefer to lead a group rather than follow during this period, and they should find ways to do so without stepping on others' toes. As well, a better way to achieve goals during this period Is to work steadfast with sincerity along with others and maintain and develop their network. They will have more energy than usual and could be successful in organising projects. Their humanitarian impulse may get stimulated. The role they play for other people in life could become the focus.

Mars Transits the Twelfth House

During this transit one could experience loss of wealth, unwanted and uncalled for expenditure. There could be some misunderstandings or friction with a partner, some disagreements with co-workers, mental worries, eye troubles, bilious and digestive complaints, troubles through those of opposite sex. This is a difficult transit if not handled properly especially if the birth chart shows affliction to planets in this house, and would be a time of frustration,
Self-denial and no credit for any good done for others. The individual could be irritable and uneasy during this period and when she/he tries to make an impression upon others or assert themselves and may draw a wrong impression upon others and under mining one's own

position. Some people who could be opposed to one's views could create some troubles. If the person feels emotionally upset, best would be to refrain from any type of significant confrontation with others, and would be a best time to work alone as much as possible, and help others, getting in to charitable activity will be suitable, research activities would be supportive along with writing and publishing. The person should plan her/his projects which they can undertake when Mars exits the transit of the twelfth house. This would be an ideal time to research and reflect upon one's goals. It can be a time when past actions catch up with the individual and this may not necessarily be a negative situation and could be a positive as well especially if Mars is benefic in the natal chart. It could also be a time when much of one's energy is channelled into private matters, or when they prefer that others do not observe what they are doing. Unconscious behaviour patterns could influence the way one asserts themselves. There could be insomnia experiences during this transit or may enjoy a more active life and, if allowed to run free, their imagination can serve them well, especially with regards to goals and new concepts.

Chapter 13

Transit of Venus

The transit of Venus being a fast moving planet is brief in every house. As some charts ore drawn with unequal houses, and also because Venus is sometimes retrograde and has an elliptical orbit, thus the length of Venus' transit duration in a house varies. However, on average, Venus transits a house for approximately 20-25 days. Venus Indicates spontaneous power of attraction between two individuals along with love and emotions, which brings the people together without any force or compulsion. It also indicates the power behind creativity, and it also indicates creation of something spiritually higher than the original entity but in this case the benefic effect and support of Mars needs to be present.

Venus indicates good effects when transits in 1st, 2nd, 3rd, 4th, 5th, 8th, 9th, 10th and 12th houses. The transits of Venus to 6th, 7th and 11th houses from natal Moon are not considered quite favourable, however the maleficence reduces with corresponding Vedhas. Venus is never more than two signs away from the Sun, and often is found in the same or neighbouring house as the Sun. In transit Venus acts to make us more receptive and cooperative in the areas of life ruled by the house it transits.

Venus indicates social life of individuals and also the one which indicates happy social occasions. Parties, entertainments, fun etc. are mostly enjoyed by people during this transit. Friendships are more enjoyable. Love is indicated by Venus, and this transit would be a good time for existing and creation of new relations. This is a good transit for finances.
Some transits of Venus also indicate some negative effects and a dull period, except when Venus Transits in conjunction with Saturn.

Venus Transits the First House

This transit of Venus spans for the stated period of around three weeks influencing the individual's style of expressions and communication for every type of engagement, be it relationships, pleasures, happiness etc. This period is good for personal compromise and contests are better avoided during this time. The person would enjoy peace with others, good food, sound sleep, dresses, perfumes, articles of luxury, enjoyment of martial relations. This period can also indicate success in education, new position and status etc. The individual may attract other people but should avoid manipulation with others as the influence of Venus in first house is transitory. This would be a good time to take up pleasure and leisure travels and engagements. The person could find it hard to deny themselves any enjoyment during this period. This is a time when a person naturally lets loose her/his softer, receptive side. Romantic matters, as well as pleasure-seeking activities, take precedence during this time. He/she is more likely to pay closer attention to their physical appearance and mannerisms, aiming to improve and enhance their personality and attractiveness. People in general find the person agreeable and cooperative during this transit duration.

Venus Transits the Second House

The transit of Venus through the second house is a good transit for finances and material possessions. The person may gain of money but they need to control their expenses and spending, as there could be spontaneous desire to spend for pleasures during this time. If money is borrowed during this transit they would be able to settle the credits. Investment can be advantageous especially in beauty and pleasure articles however the same may be avoided in routine and mundane articles. They will have happiness at home, happiness with family, could also receive some gifts and would have all round prosperity. Will be able to maintain good health and will remain in good spirits. As the natural ruler of this house of the chart, Venus is a natural benefic here. This is a good position for Venus, although there would be some restlessness when it comes to money and expenses. Financial security and enjoyment of the good things in life would take the precedence during this time, although the person could value simple pleasures. The ability to relate well with others might enhance their own personal finances during this period. The person could find themselves in a position in which there would be a blending of financial matters with social or public affairs. This is a stable position for matters of love and close relationships. The individual would value those who make her/him feel comfortable, and familiarity is more important to them.

Venus Transits the Third House

The person would be mostly cheerful in her/his approach to others, and also could be somewhat intellectual, during this transit. Especially, the individual would be quite a good companion with everyone he/she comes across. They will enjoy talking about what interests them, and will find great value in the exchange of ideas. Sometimes this transit brings benefit through siblings, communications, or short trips. During this period, he/she will be attracted to wit, cheerfulness, and verbal rapport. They will be especially good at mediating conflicts, smoothing over differences using their diplomacy skills. All activities will be more pleasant and agreeable. Social life combined with parties, get-togethers will be more enjoyable. They need to try and avoid to be serious during this transit duration. They could gain from their business or profession. This would be a time of love and harmony.

This transit also indicates prosperity, happiness, gain of wealth, success, favour and profits from friends and relations. Increased influence and honour. Gain of luxury articles, good pleasures and loveable company.

Venus Transits the Fourth House

During this transit there will be domestic happiness and comforts, of conducive nature and a happy atmosphere in the family. Good relations with family and elders, indications of better earnings, comforts, improvement or some good changes in home, pleasant journeys, and the person should take care for food against digestive troubles. Increased power and influence, gains from business and/or profession. Pleasure trips and comforts with some good news can be expected. During this transit, the person would especially be fond of the life at home and family. The person will be more receptive and gentle with family, friends and colleagues, and tend to be sentimental or nostalgic. They may particularly value the aesthetics in and around their home during this period. If things are not conducive on the home front, the person will do whatever she/he can to create a peaceful and stable atmosphere. Loyalty and sensitivity in relationships are more important to the person than other times, during this transit duration. They might focus on ways to earn money from properties or conveyances. This transit would have a calming influence when simple pleasures appeal the most.

Venus Transits the Fifth House

During this transit the individual can expect happiness from elders and children. Children would make the parents and elders proud by their performance. There could be advantageous position in many situations whether in professional or in family lives. Friends and colleagues will be helpful. The individual would feel like helping out those in need especially the under-privileged. This transit duration is a good time for entertainment, amusement as well as affairs of children. Love relationships will be favourable, and smooth with loved ones. This is an expressive period for the love relationships and romance. It's natural for the person to turn on the charm without even a second thought. The individual will be especially attracted to aesthetic forms of recreation and would feel a little more playful during this period. Matters of love tend to be laced with a touch of drama. More loving and appreciative relationships with one's children may also figure during this time. The powers of attraction skyrocket during this time and people will generally get attracted to the charm of this individual. Creative expression of any kind is favourable during this time and one instinctively knows how to place themselves in the best light in order to make a good impression on others. Any love affair which commences during this transit duration will be characterized by good cheer, fun, and a fair share of lasting emotional connection.

Venus Transits the Sixth House

During this transit, the individual may confront difficulties, as this transit of Venus is not quite conducive from some perspectives. There could be irritation due to unavoidable reasons and circumstances and there could be anxiety. Problems in relationship could also be there. There could be some positive developments with respect to service and good rapport with
In professional and business environment. There will be positive influence on health, however it better to avoid over eating. This transit is not quite favourable position for romance. Establishing a happy and harmonious work environment through friendly relations with co-workers or tidying up one's work area comes into focus.
The person is generally well liked and respected socially on the professional front during this

transit. There could be lethargy in the routine during this period. There is likelihood of having good team spirit during this transit and the person will be more tactful and obliging with his/her co-workers. He/she will be less inclined to take ahead relationship matters. The person will be successful doing and undertaking tasks that involve cooperation and team harmony. The person could find that her/his talents or skills are especially appreciated.

Venus Transits the Seventh House

This transit of Venus through the seventh house is a good position for all relationships, Jove affairs, and romance with partner, wife and cordial relations with co-workers etc. The person may get married if unmarried, during this time. The individual would be able to express his/her feelings of love and affection to the partner, beloved, superiors etc. which could get reciprocated. In profession, partnership will be gainful, favourable and of mutual benefit. During this transit, if the individual in a dilemma of relationships or conflict due to any relationships in life, this is the best time for rapprochement. During this transit duration, even those thoroughly opposed to the person would be receptive and may react positively if approached correctly and amicably. During this transit there would be good chance of settling down disputes outside courts of law. Special attention to and from would be in focus, and praising and keeping the partner happy could get the individual everywhere if used wisely. One-to-one relating appeals to the person more than group activities or more casual connections. Smoothing out one's close personal relationships would give happiness during this time. If single, the individual would be more willing to enter into a committed relationship. In general, the individual will be adaptable when it comes to affections and willing to compromise, negotiate, and make peace.

Venus Transits the Eighth House

During this transit of Venus through the eighth house, there could be gain of wealth through spouse, or business partner or bank or financial institutions. Union or re-union with partner, wife/husband or beloved can happen. The health would remain generally normal. Love relations started during this transit time will be lasting one. There could be chance of gaining something through property. There would be happiness and pleasure through opposite sex, domestic bliss, fame, honour, all round prosperity etc. During this transit, a financial boost is possible, or the person may gain financially through her/his partner. A deep and intimate connection made during this period could be revitalizing and even healing. The individual would be more inclined to want to smooth over differences in a partnership concerning the sharing of power, intimacy matters, finances, and other emotionally-connected matters of interest. Intimate relationships could get intensified during this time. Either the person or her/his partner may start to improve the relationship as a lifetime goal.

Venus Transits the Ninth House

During this transit of Venus through the ninth house there could be indications of good deeds and friendly relations, some gains, mental happiness, likelihood of enjoyable romance and comforts. For those eligible they may get married, enjoy distant travels with loved ones. Blessings of elders would be there. The person could get a chance to gain knowledge towards the path of fame and prosperity. Love relations will give good experience. The person could get attracted to a stranger, may be a foreigner or at strange place, better educated and experienced than the person, which will be quite helpful and gainful. This transit also indicates. a taste for the exotic encounters. Routine affairs simply don't seem to satisfy the individual and he/she would be on a lookout for something extraordinary and exciting. The person receives pleasure from anything that expands her/his horizons, both physically and mentally. Foreign people and places may particularly appeal during this period and will tend to be expansive and generous when it comes to love. A love interest to whom one gets attracted during this transit time may be somebody who the person previously wouldn't have considered attractive, or someone whose cultural background could be quite different. The person will have a taste for the exotic and the spirit to match. Public relations work, promotion, and other such endeavours would be favoured during this time. It is more about how one expresses themselves rather than the specifics during this time. There could be special rapport with people from distant places or foreign contacts and with the opposite sex. The person will be more attractive and charming during this transit period, which increases one's popularity. If a romance were to begin during this time, it is more likely to be with someone of a different background or educational level, or someone who comes across during travel. She/he would have a taste for the exotic during this phase that can show up in many areas of life. Life would seem quite meaningful and the person would be able to work towards achieving his/her objectives and in some cases they could even achieve their goals.

Venus Transits the Tenth House

This a favourable transit for business and profession. Persons in authority could be favourable and helpful to the individual. Relation with elders and would be helpful with superiors, business and professional colleagues. The person also needs to be careful of some relationships who could be hidden opponents and will try to ruin the reputation, which could in turn spoil the relations and may bring obstacles, impediments, irritation and humiliations, conflicts and law suits etc. During this transit the individual could be charming and well-received on the professional front. Their responsibility and authority would be likeable qualities, making this a favourable period overall for those in a higher position, as well as for negotiations or social activities related to profession or business. The presence of Venus in the tenth house which is the professional domain showers charm and an affectionate nature and could also benefit in career and social opportunities. The person will be socially ambitious during this transit and would be successful in profession and may excel due to good managerial qualities or some form of artistic talent or, indirectly through either the business partner or life partner. The individual could also come across people who could be highly skilled and competent and may get opportunity to learn.

Venus Transits the Eleventh House

During this transit there could be bonding with harmonious and warm social friends. The person may meet someone important through social contacts or activities. There could be chance of also sharing of thoughts not just on material level but also on philosophical direction during this time. The transit of Venus in the eleventh house enlivens the individual's friendships and group associations with charm and grace. He/she would be more peace-loving than usual and could be slightly detached on a personal level. If a romance were to begin during this time frame, it would be characterized by a strong feeling of bonding and togetherness, but it could also be rather impersonal and perhaps may lack in depth. Gain through friends could be there, association with opposite sex, mental and domestic happiness, gain of some money and prosperity could be there. The person would be happy at home and also there would be increase in earnings. This would be one of the good times for team or group work, and being friendly to all parties and pleasure pursuits. Mostly people will be affectionate in any sphere. All love relations previous or new will be lasting.

Venus Transits the Twelfth House

During this transit Venus is posited in the privacy domain of the individual indicating hibernation, which further points that the affection towards a loved one is expressed after a good evaluation and analysis. Attraction to secrets and whispers characterise this period, although for some, it can also be a time of endings and relationship concerns. Personal and social contacts could be secretive, and there can be secret love affairs, or at least very private love feelings and longings. Shyness can lead to some loneliness or romantic frustration. In the twelfth house this is a good transit of Venus. It indicates gain of things and enjoyment, luxury, increased expenditure and pleasures of beds. There could be some gains however minor in nature, some investments and improvements. The person would be inclined to get involved in some charitable activity, be helpful to others and especially to the loved ones. Should try not to inflict sarcastic remarks and hurl insults as these would boomerang for sure. Also should avoid giving false hopes to others. On the whole, this transit will be good and rewarding. Twelfth house indicates spiritualism and Venus tends to take away that from the individual towards material comforts, needs and luxuries and the individual should take care against being drawn in to these.